Contents

III Route planning

1 Road maps

41 Town and city plans

54 Index to road maps

Patent applied for.

Cartography by Philip's
Copyright © 2000 George Philip Ltd

First published as *Philip's Britain & Ireland Road Atlas* in 1996 by George Philip Ltd.
a division of Octopus Publishing Group Limited
2-4 Heron Quays, London E14 4JP

Sixth Edition 2000

Published in 2001 by Tuffmap™
Trade enquires 0151 474 5510.

ISBN: 0-9541459-0-9

Printed by Norwich Colour Print.

Road map symbols

Abbreviated local authority areas

(BD)	Bridgend	9	U16
(BF)	Bracknell Forest	6	V22
(BG)	Blaenau Gwent	9	U17
(BH)	Brighton and Hove	6	W23
(BL)	Blackpool	15	Q17
(BM)	Bournemouth	5	W20
(BN)	Blackburn with Darwen	15	Q19
(CB)	City of Bristol	4	V18
(CE)	City of Edinburgh	25	L17
(CF)	Cardiff	4	U17
(CM)	Clackmannanshire	24	K16
(CN)	City of Nottingham	11	S21
(CY)	Caerphilly	4	U17
(DD)	Dundee City	25	K18
(DE)	Derby City	11	S21
(DN)	Darlington	16	N20
(ED)	East Dunbartonshire	19	L15
(ER)	East Renfrewshire	19	L15
(FK)	Falkirk	24	L16
(GC)	Glasgow City	19	L15
(HL)	Hartlepool	21	N21
(HN)	Halton	15	R18
(IC)	Inverclyde	19	L14
(KH)	Kingston upon Hull	17	Q23
(LE)	Leicester City	11	S21
(LU)	Luton	12	U23
(MB)	Middlesbrough	16	N21
(MR)	Merthyr Tydfil	9	U17
(NEL)	North East Lincolnshire	17	Q23
(NL)	North Lanarkshire	19	L16
(NP)	Newport	4	U18
(NPT)	Neath Port Talbot	9	U16
(PL)	Plymouth	3	X15
(PM)	Portsmouth	5	W21
(PO)	Poole	5	W20
(RC)	Redcar and Cleveland	17	N22
(RD)	Reading	6	V22
(RF)	Renfrewshire	19	L14
(RT)	Rhondda Cynon Taff	9	U17
(SD)	Southend-on-Sea	7	U25
(SL)	Slough	6	U22
(SN)	Stockton-on-Tees	21	N21
(SO)	Southampton	5	W21
(ST)	Stoke-on-Trent	10	R19
(SW)	Swindon	5	U20
(TB)	Torbay	3	X16
(TF)	Torfaen	4	U17
(TK)	Thurrock	7	U24
(TW)	Telford and Wrekin	10	S19
(WA)	Warrington	15	R18
(WD)	West Dunbartonshire	24	L15
(WK)	Wokingham	6	V22
(WL)	West Lothian	24	L16
(WM)	Windsor & Maidenhead	6	V22

Motorway

junction – full / restricted access

service area – full / restricted access

under construction

Primary route – dual / single carriageway

under construction

DERBY   primary destination

A road / national secondary road

under construction

B road / regional road

under construction

Other road

Major Distance (in miles)

Minor Distance (in miles)

Tunnel

Railway

International boundary

National boundary

County / local authority boundary

River

Canal

Lake / reservoir

Car ferry

Hovercraft

Major airport

Built-up area

National park, forest park, area of outstanding natural beauty

1342   Spot height in metres

Scale

0	5	10	15	20	25 miles

0	5	10	15	20	25	30	35	40 km

12 miles to 1 inch, 1:760320

England map — Route Planner

0   20   40 Miles
0   20   40   60 Km

Sanquhar, Moffat, A74, A7, A697, A1
Dumfries, A75, Gretna, Morpeth, Ashington
Castle Douglas, Carlisle, Hexham, Gateshead, Tynemouth
Newcastle-upon-Tyne, South Shields
A69, A696, A692, **Sunderland**
Workington, Keswick, Penrith, Washington, Durham, Hartlepool
Whitehaven, A66, A68, A1(M)
A595, Brough, **Stockton-on-Tees**, Redcar
Ambleside, Windermere, A66, Darlington, **Middlesbrough**, Whitby
Kendal, A685, A19, A171
Barrow-in-Furness, **E N G L A N D**, Thirsk, Scarborough
Morecambe, Lancaster, Ripon, A170, A165
Fleetwood, A65, Skipton, Harrogate, York, A166, Bridlington
Blackpool, Clitheroe, A59, Wetherby, A64
Preston, Keighley, **Leeds**, Selby, A614, **Kingston upon Hull**
Southport, Blackburn, **Bradford**, Dewsbury, Goole, Immingham
Crosby, Wigan, **Bolton**, Halifax, Rochdale, Wakefield, **Huddersfield**, Scunthorpe, Grimsby
St. Helens, Salford, Oldham, Barnsley, Doncaster, A180
Wallasey, **Liverpool**, **Manchester**, **Stockport**, Rotherham, A15, Gainsborough, A16
Birkenhead, **Warrington**, Sale, **Sheffield**, Worksop, Lincoln, A158, Skegness
Conwy, Ellesmere Port, Macclesfield, Chesterfield, A57
Bangor, Queensferry, Northwich, Buxton, Mansfield, Newark-on-Trent, A52, The Wash, Cromer
Betws-y-Coed, Chester, Crewe, Leek, Matlock, A60, Sleaford, Boston, A148
Llangollen, Whitchurch, Congleton, **Stoke-on-Trent**, **Derby**, **Nottingham**, Grantham, Spalding, King's Lynn, **Norwich**, Great Yarmouth
Oswestry, A49, Newcastle-under-Lyme, Loughborough, A17, Wisbech, Swaffham, Lowestoft
Welshpool, Shrewsbury, A41, Stafford, Burton-upon-Trent, Melton Mowbray, Stamford, Downham Market, A11, A140, Beccles
Newtown, A54, Lichfield, **Leicester**, Oakham, A47, Peterborough, Thetford, Diss, A143
Telford, **Walsall**, A511, Corby, A605, A1(M), Ely, Bury St. Edmunds, Ipswich
Wolverhampton, **West Bromwich**, **Coventry**, Kettering, Huntingdon, Newmarket, A14
Dudley, **Birmingham**, **Solihull**, **Northampton**, Wellingborough, Cambridge, A134, **Ipswich**
Kidderminster, Redditch, Warwick, St. Neots, Bedford, Sudbury, Felixstowe, Harwich
Rhayader, Leominster, Worcester, Stratford-upon-Avon, A428, A45, A423, A5, Colchester, Clacton-on-Sea
Builth Wells, Llandrindod Wells, Hereford, Evesham, Banbury, **Milton Keynes**, **Luton**, Stevenage, Bishop's Stortford, A120
Llandovery, Ledbury, **Luton**, Dunstable, St. Albans, A1(M), Hertford, Chelmsford, **Basildon**
Brecon, Ross-on-Wye, Cheltenham, A41, Aylesbury, Hemel Hempstead, Harlow, Brentwood
Abergavenny, Monmouth, Gloucester, Cirencester, Oxford, High Wycombe, Watford, M25, **Southend-on-Sea**
Merthyr Tydfil, Cwmbran, Chepstow, Stroud, A419, Swindon, A40, Slough, **LONDON**, Tilbury, Sheerness, Margate
Neath, Port Talbot, M4, M48, M5, A429, Reading, Staines, Croydon, Gillingham, Ramsgate
Newport, **Bristol**, Chippenham, Newbury, Bracknell, Esher, Reigate, Sevenoaks, Maidstone, Canterbury
Bridgend, **Cardiff**, Bath, A350, A33, Woking, East Grinstead, Ashford, Dover, Folkestone
Weston-super-Mare, Shepton Mallet, Trowbridge, Warminster, Basingstoke, Farnham, Guildford, Crawley, Royal Tunbridge Wells, Hawkhurst, A259
Minehead, Frome, Andover, Alton, Petersfield, Horsham, A22, Hastings
Barnstaple, Glastonbury, Salisbury, Winchester, Eastleigh, Midhurst, Chichester, Lewes, Hove, Eastbourne
Bideford, Taunton, Yeovil, Blandford Forum, **Southampton**, Fareham, Worthing, Newhaven, **Brighton**
Exeter, Okehampton, A303, Ringwood, **Poole**, Dorchester, **Portsmouth**, Bognor Regis, Gosport
Tavistock, Torquay, Paignton, Exmouth, Weymouth, **Bournemouth**, Isle of Wight
Plymouth

Channel *ENGLISH CHANNEL*

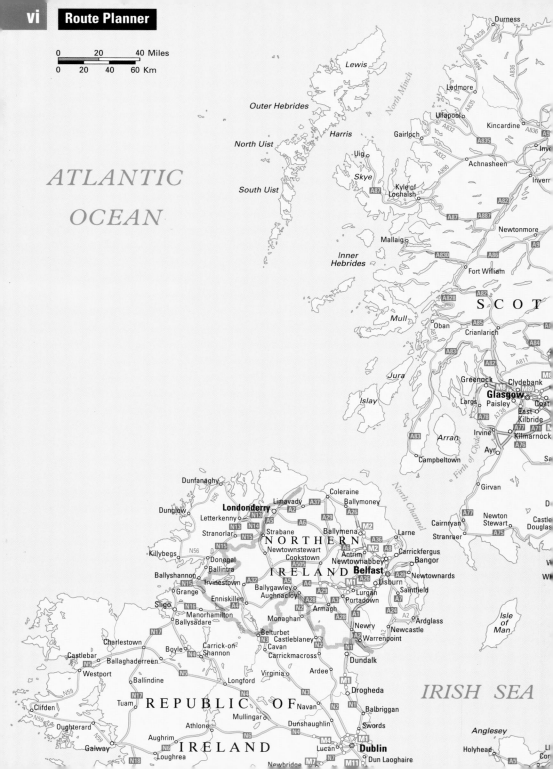

0   20   40 Miles

0   20   40   60 Km

rso

Wick

A9

A99

9

Moray Firth

Fraserburgh

don   Elgin

A98

Peterhead

96

A96

A90

A95

A93

Aberdeen

Braemar

NORTH

SEA

A93

Montrose

Forfar

A90

A92

Arbroath

A N D

Perth

A90

Dundee

A92

St. Andrews

A90

M90

Glenrothes

A91

ling   A92   Kirkcaldy

Firth of Forth

Falkirk   Dunfermline

M9

Edinburgh   A1

bernauld   M8

e A71   Livingston   A68

Berwick-upon-Tweed

herwell   A702

A72   Peebles   Coldstream

A703

A7   Galashiels

A702

Hawick   A68   Jedburgh   Alnwick

Moffat   A7   A697   A1

76   Ashington

es   A74(M)   Morpeth   A696

A75   **Newcastle-upon-Tyne**   Tynemouth

Gretna   A69   Hexham   Gateshead   South Shields

Carlisle   A692   **Sunderland**

Washington

A596   Durham   A19   Hartlepool

A68

M6   A1(M)   Redcar

gton   A66   Keswick   Penrith   **Stockton-on-Tees**

aven   A66   Brough   **Middlesbrough**   Whitby

A595   A66   Darlington   A171

A591   A685   A66

Ambleside   Thirsk   A170   Scarborough

Windermere   A1

Kendal   A19   A165

w-in-Furness   A590   Ripon   A64   Bridlington

E N G L A N D

A61   A1(M)

Morecambe   A65   Harrogate   York   A166

Lancaster   M6   Skipton   A59   Wetherby

Fleetwood   Clitheroe   Keighley

Blackpool   A585   M55   **Bradford**   **Leeds**   Selby   A614   **Kingston upon Hull**

M55   Burnley   Halifax   Dewsbury

Preston   Blackburn   M62   Wakefield   Goole   Immingham

Southport   M61   Rochdale   **Huddersfield**   A15   Grimsby

Crosby   M58   **Bolton**   Bury   Oldham   Barnsley   Doncaster   Scunthorpe   A46

St. Helens   Salford   A628   M1   A16

Wallasey   M62   **Manchester**   Rotherham   Gainsborough

dno   **Liverpool**   Sale   **Stockport**   **Sheffield**   A631

Birkenhead   M53   A57   Warrington   M56   Macclesfield   Chesterfield   A1   Lincoln   A158   Skegness

A55   Ellesmere Port   Runcorn   Northwich   M6   Buxton   A6   A614   Mansfield

A61   A57

HOW TO USE THIS TABLE

Distances are shown in miles

Example: the distance from Cambridge to Dover is 125 miles

Cambridge 169
Cardiff 190 45
Carlisle 289 264 277
Dover 389 238 125 202
Dundee 523 152 441 406 430

London
Aberdeen 517
Aberystwyth 445 211
Birmingham 114 420 117
Bournemouth 147 207 564 107
Brighton 92 163 253 573 52
Bristol 147 82 81 125 493 122
Cambridge 169 116 154 100 214 471 54
Cardiff 190 45 182 117 103 105 505 157
Carlisle 289 264 277 370 343 196 224 221 301
Dover 389 238 125 202 82 174 194 292 588 71
Dundee 523 152 441 406 430 517 495 349 376 67 448
Edinburgh 56 462 96 385 345 373 456 439 292 320 125 390
Fishguard 399 460 331 297 112 270 154 291 222 170 56 504 260
Fort William 486 144 127 596 206 485 479 486 575 539 392 430 149 510
Glasgow 101 376 44 83 488 96 385 372 373 468 439 292 320 145 397
Gloucester 346 454 153 349 410 191 247 56 123 35 159 99 56 102 468 109
Harwich 196 432 543 337 413 469 125 336 246 67 217 128 187 167 281 535 76
Holyhead 349 191 330 438 167 333 394 360 231 216 270 206 334 288 148 111 439 269
Inverness 474 569 504 166 66 542 158 132 622 262 549 505 539 617 597 458 486 105 550
John o' Groats 129 603 693 628 295 195 671 285 259 747 391 680 630 668 741 724 574 601 232 663
Kingston upon Hull 518 394 231 196 198 254 369 280 234 295 256 158 244 139 233 245 264 134 223 364 184
Land's End 421 868 741 405 390 235 573 686 353 574 642 381 477 245 374 200 308 205 281 313 692 297
Leeds 405 55 487 360 176 223 174 215 329 237 202 258 260 119 232 145 194 260 255 113 169 327 189
Lincoln 68 371 44 554 427 216 155 159 291 399 272 258 314 202 191 208 85 183 197 209 90 199 383 131
Liverpool 129 75 361 130 511 382 102 265 140 216 329 160 216 286 299 120 165 194 161 272 234 93 104 341 202
Manchester 35 84 40 361 95 500 373 124 228 126 215 329 197 215 285 276 119 183 165 161 257 227 80 129 340 185
Newcastle upon Tyne 132 168 159 92 498 132 395 268 272 308 266 148 253 329 110 166 358 57 325 241 299 352 347 207 257 235 286
Norwich 264 185 220 105 176 421 149 654 529 311 73 204 385 504 343 366 422 174 289 262 62 252 175 214 166 276 496 114
Oban 492 233 307 308 387 307 665 346 244 117 427 524 441 92 49 481 123 117 585 188 477 468 465 565 530 384 412 178 499
Oxford 462 145 260 144 172 137 168 274 192 656 532 238 145 52 356 472 205 372 433 141 260 108 83 74 108 90 64 154 483 57
Plymouth 199 587 343 410 283 283 293 316 89 355 790 664 328 309 157 495 595 264 496 552 300 399 167 293 122 224 128 203 237 615 218
Sheffield 283 135 339 146 125 38 72 46 33 361 65 520 393 168 187 126 248 348 215 235 291 245 152 194 120 161 226 216 76 159 360 159
Shrewsbury 82 225 106 364 205 201 69 58 133 109 303 169 567 438 113 240 77 272 382 145 274 330 251 176 111 159 103 226 185 45 77 399 160
Southampton 185 199 151 64 530 206 324 221 239 204 232 228 256 723 598 293 164 105 433 541 233 438 500 143 324 121 148 76 61 31 128 201 547 77
Stranraer 445 277 263 500 379 148 403 158 220 221 298 220 585 259 379 262 338 435 343 84 195 392 124 167 496 101 390 379 378 475 444 297 325 228 402
Swansea 417 161 118 217 206 141 506 301 347 187 195 233 248 285 264 696 572 184 267 89 409 496 67 412 473 274 309 41 227 85 222 167 119 73 507 194
York 272 222 258 133 52 333 181 309 181 84 64 99 75 24 411 37 479 352 204 228 189 217 330 261 194 250 282 121 244 165 222 275 269 130 195 319 207

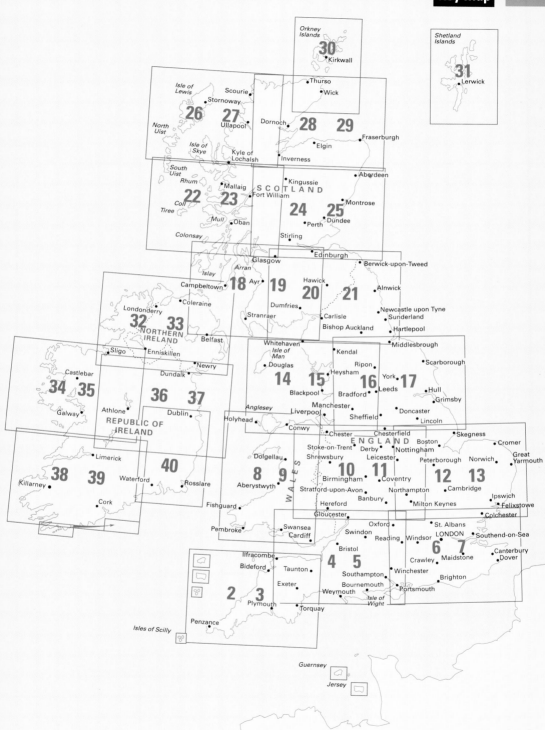

Orkney Islands

30 Kirkwall

Shetland Islands

31 Lerwick

Thurso

Wick

Isle of Lewis

Scourie

Stornoway

26 **27** Dornoch **28** **29** Fraserburgh

North Uist Ullapool

Elgin

Isle of Skye

Kyle of Lochalsh Inverness

Aberdeen

South Uist

Rhum Mallaig Kingussie

22 **23** Fort William SCOTLAND

Coll

Tiree Mull **24** Montrose

Colonsay Oban **25** Dundee

Perth

Stirling

Glasgow Edinburgh

Islay Arran Berwick-upon-Tweed

Campbeltown **18** Ayr **19** Hawick Alnwick

20 **21**

Dumfries Newcastle upon Tyne

Londonderry Stranraer Carlisle Sunderland

Coleraine Bishop Auckland Hartlepool

32 **33** Belfast Middlesbrough

NORTHERN IRELAND Whitehaven

Sligo Enniskillen Isle of Man Kendal Scarborough

Newry Ripon

Castlebar Dundalk Douglas Heysham York Hull

34 **35** **36** **37** **14** **15** **16** **17** Grimsby

Galway Athlone Dublin Blackpool Bradford Leeds

REPUBLIC OF Anglesey Manchester Doncaster Lincoln

Limerick IRELAND Holyhead Liverpool Sheffield

Conwy Chester Chesterfield Skegness

38 **39** **40** Waterford Chester England Boston Cromer

Killarney Rosslare Dolgellau Stoke-on-Trent Derby Nottingham Great Yarmouth

Cork Shrewsbury Leicester Peterborough Norwich

Fishguard **8** **9** Birmingham **10** **11** Coventry **12** **13**

Aberystwyth Stratford-upon-Avon Northampton Cambridge

Pembroke WALES Hereford Banbury Milton Keynes Ipswich

Gloucester Felixstowe

Swansea Oxford St. Albans Colchester

Ilfracombe Cardiff Swindon LONDON

Bideford Reading Windsor **6** **7** Southend-on-Sea

4 **5** Bristol Crawley Maidstone Canterbury

Taunton Winchester Dover

Exeter Southampton Brighton

2 **3** Bournemouth Portsmouth

Weymouth Isle of Wight

Plymouth Torquay

Penzance

Isles of Scilly

Guernsey

Jersey

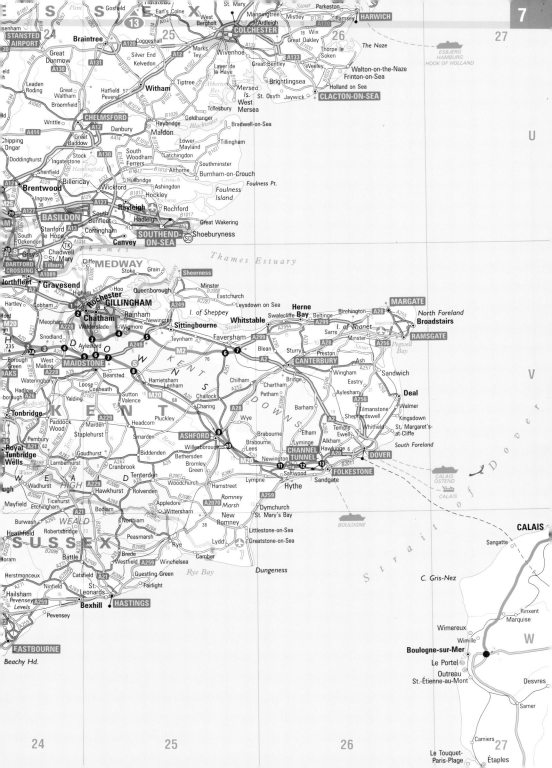

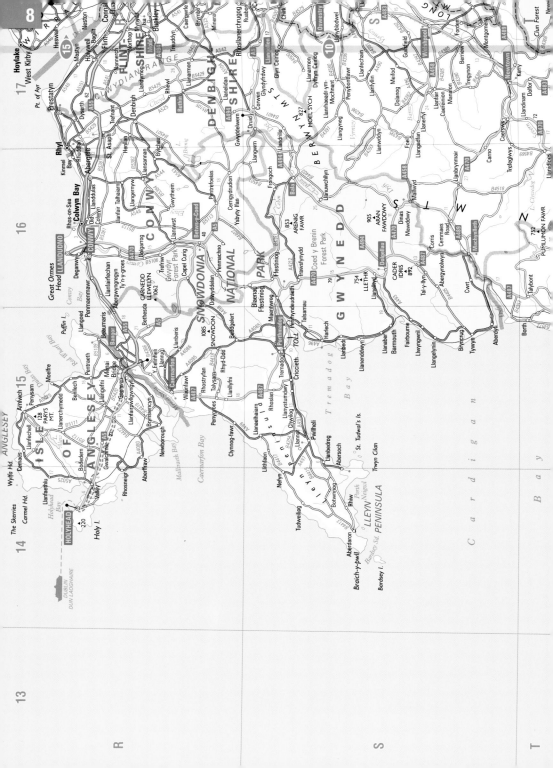

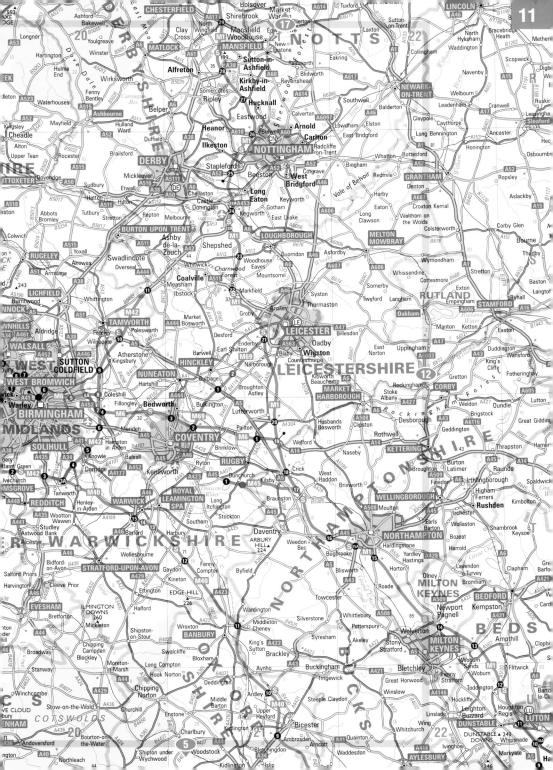

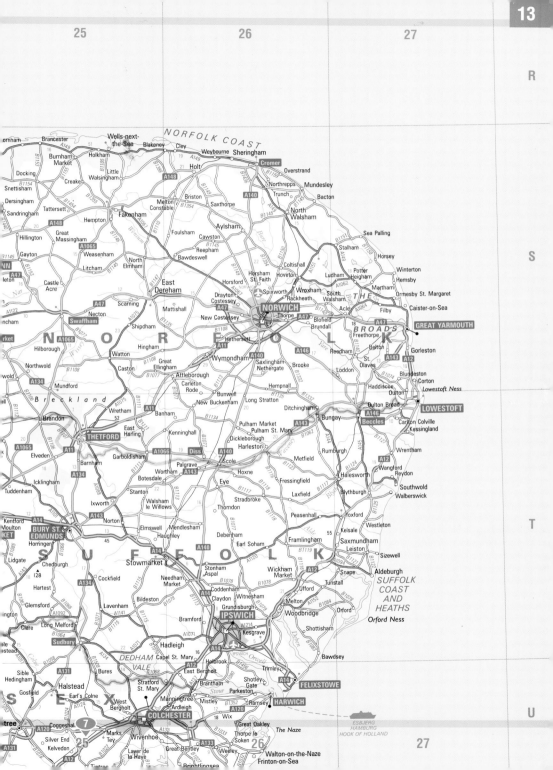

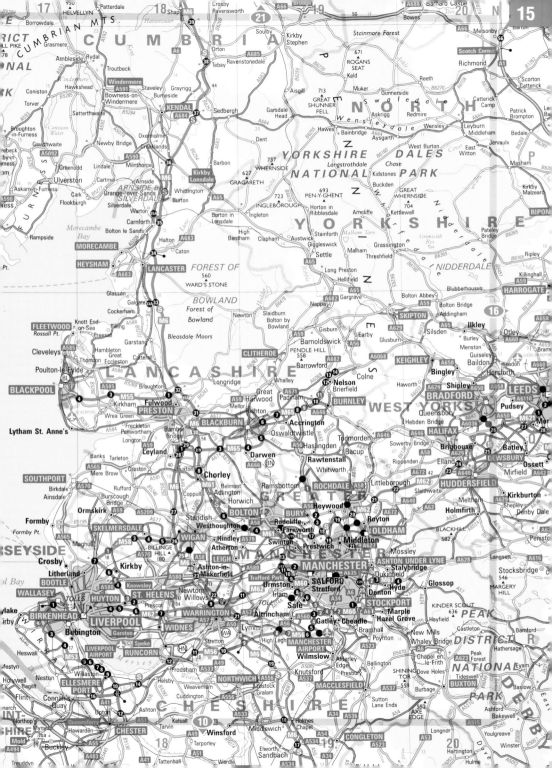

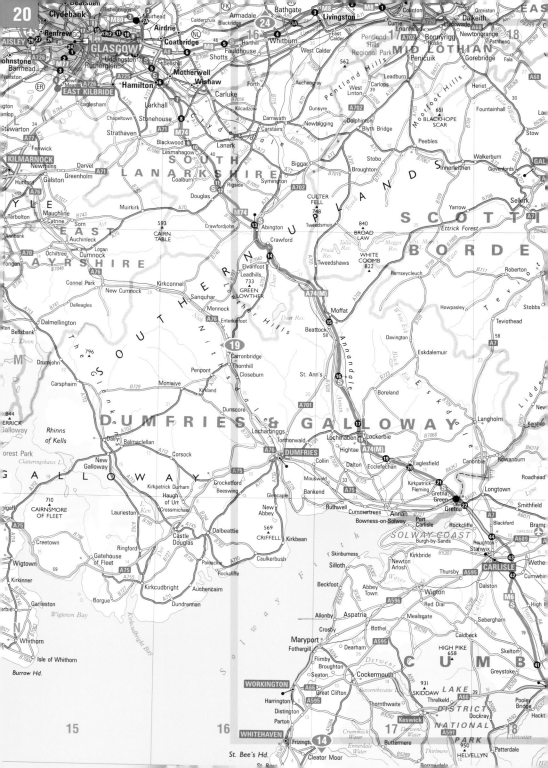

8   9   10   11

H

J

K

L

8   9   10   11

26

18

SOUTH

Rubha Ardvule

BEN MHOR
620

UIST

Dalabrog
A865
Loch Baghasdail
(Lochboisdale)
L. Boisdale
B888

Cille Bhrighde

Sound of Eriskay

Eriskay

Sound of Barra

Greian Hd.

A888
BARRA
HEAVAL
384

Bruernish Pt.

Bagh a Chaisteil
(Castlebay)

Vatersay

Sandray

Pabbay

Mingulay

Berneray

MINGINISH   SKYE
Sligachan   GLAMAIG
CUILLIN
Glenbrittle   HILLS   928
1009   BLA
BHEINN

*Rubh'a
Dunain*

Canna

Sanday

Soay

Elgol

Tarskava

Pt. of
Sleat

Kilmory
RÙM   Kinloch
Harris   810

Cleadale
394   Eigg
Galmisdale
Sd. of Eigg

Muck

Cuillin   Sd.
Sd. of Canna
Sound of Rhum

Kilmory
Achosnich
Pt. of
Ardnamurchan   ARDNAMU
Kilchoan   BEN H
Mingary

Sorisdale
B8072
COLL
Clabhach   *B8071*
Annagour
B8070
Acha

TIREE
B8069   Caoles
Middleton   Scarinish   *B8068*
Hynish B.
Hynish

Passage   of   Tiree

Tobermory
Caliach
Pt.   Calgary   Dervaig   *B8073*
L. Frisa
Oskamull
Treshnish
Is.   L. Tuath   *B8073*
Gometra   Ulva   *L. na Keal*
Staffa   BEN
B8035
L. Scridain

Iona
Fionnphort   *A849*
Bunessan   ROSS OF MULL

Torran
Rocks

COLONSAY
B8086
Scalasaig
B8085

Oronsay

Passage   of   Oronsay
L. Tar

Rubh a' Mhail

Ardnave Pt.   PAPS
Ardnave   Bunnahabhain

INNER   HEBRIDES

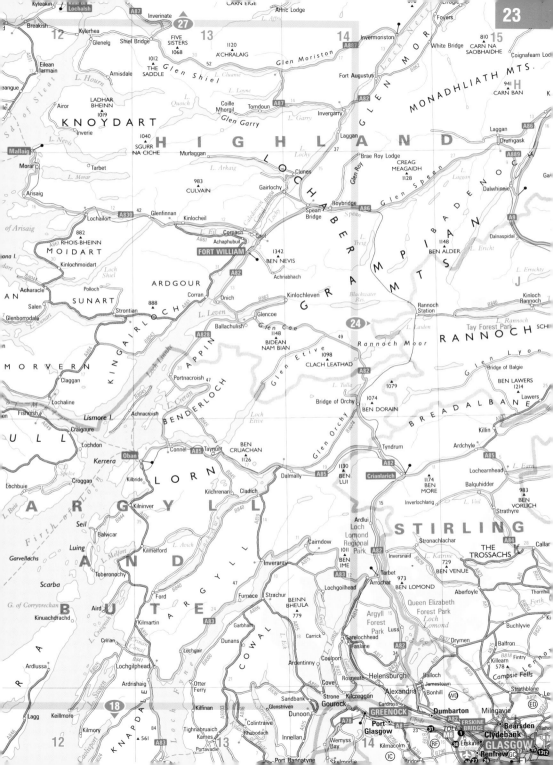

11 12 13 14

C. Wrath
Kyle of Durness
Faraid Hd.
Whiten Hd.
Achiemore
Durness
Strathan
E
Heilam A838
Kinlochbervie
Sheigra
L. Inchard
A838
Eriboll
Tongue
Rhiconich
908 ▲ FOINAVEN
927 ▲ BEN HOPE
763 ▲ BEN LOYAL
Handa I.
L. Laxford
Reay Forest
Strathmore
Scourie
Laxford Bridge
721 ▲ BEN STACK
L. More
A838
Eddrachillis Bay
873 ▲ BEN HEE
Altnaharra
Pt. of Stoer
Kylestrome
Unapool
Kinloch
F
Drumbeg
SUTHERLAND
961 ▲ BEN KLIBRECK
Culkein
809 ▲ QUINAG
Stoer
ASSYNT
Inchnadamph
998 ▲ BEN MORE ASSYNT
28
Lochinver
L. Assynt
A837
Duchally
Glen Oykel
Inverkirkaig
847 ▲ CANISP
Sallachy
Lairg
Rubha Coigeach
Enard B.
Elphin
Ledmore
To
Reiff
Achiltibuie
Lurgainn
Cromalt Hills
Lubcroy
Rosehall
A839
Altass
Inveran
Summer Is.
Achavraie
COIGACH
Strathkanaird
Oykel Bridge
Oykel
Culrain
Greenstone Pt.
Gruinard B.
L. Broom
Ardgay
Kincardine
Freewater Forest
Croick
Alt na h'Airbhe
Ullapool
Mellon Charles
Laide
Badrallach
Ardcharnich
EASTER ROSS
Cove
Aultbea
Ardessie
12
L. Eive
1062 ▲ AN TEALLACH
1081 ▲ BEN DEARG
Carron
Melvaig
L. na Sealga
A835
Braemore
G
Longa I.
Poolewe
Fionn L.
L. Glascarnoch
56
L. Glas
L. Gairloch
Gairloch
L. Maree
1109 ▲ SGURR MOR
1045 ▲ BEN WYVIS
Eva
Port Henderson
Kerrysdale
B8056
981 ▲ SLIOCH
L. Fannich
A835
Red Point
Talladale
WESTER ROSS
Garve
Strathpeffer
Dingw
Staffin
L. Torridon
Kinlochewe
A832
Achanalt
Garbe
L. Luichart
Contin
Conon
STORR 719
Rona
Diabaig
LIATHACH 1053 ▲
Achnasheen
Milton
Muir of Ord
A832
NISH
Fasag Torridon
Strathconon
Glen Orrin
D
Beauly
Shieldaig
Scardoy
THE AIRD
RAASAY
G Applecross Forest
H
Achnashellach
SGURR A' CHOIRE GHLAIS
Stroy
Beauly
Brochel
Coulags
1052 L. Monar
1083
Monar Forest
Drumnadrochit
Portree
Applecross
Kishorn
Ardarroch
Lochcarron
Monar Lodge
MEALFUARVONIE 696 ▲
Toscaig
Stromemore
A890
SGURR NA LAPAICH 1150 ▲
Liatrie
Cannich
Lewiston
Clachan
Plockton
Mullardoch
Strath Glass
Crowlin Is.
Stromeferry
Ling
A82
Sconser
Scalpay
Kyle of Lochalsh
Auchtertyre Dornie
1182 ▲ CARN EIGE
Affric Lodge
Errogie
775 ▲ GLAMAIG
12
23
Affric
MEALFUARVONIE
Foyers
Kyleakin
L. Alsh
A87
Inverinate
13
Glen Affric
14

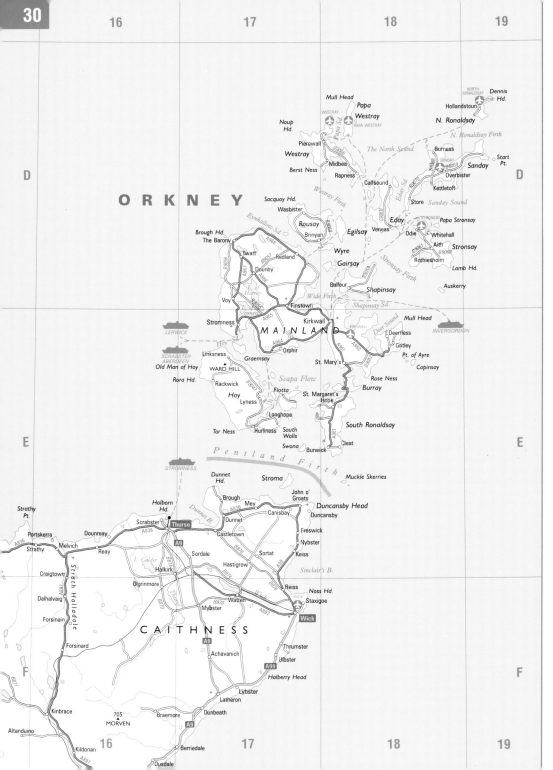

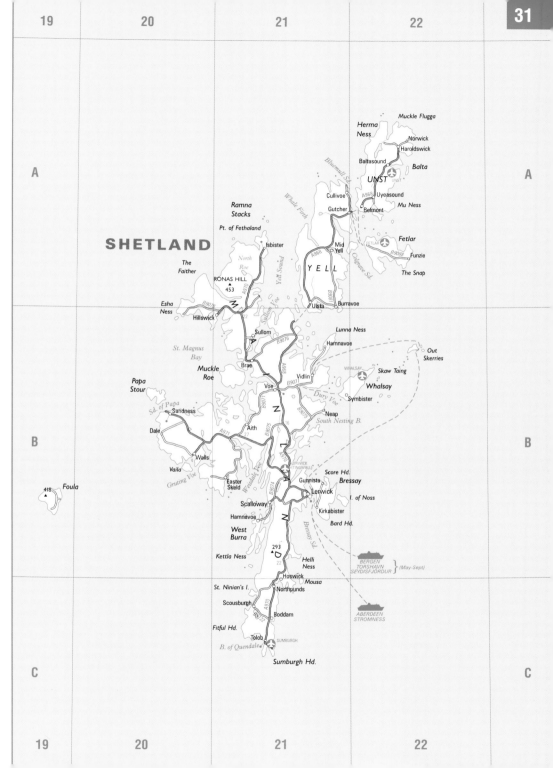

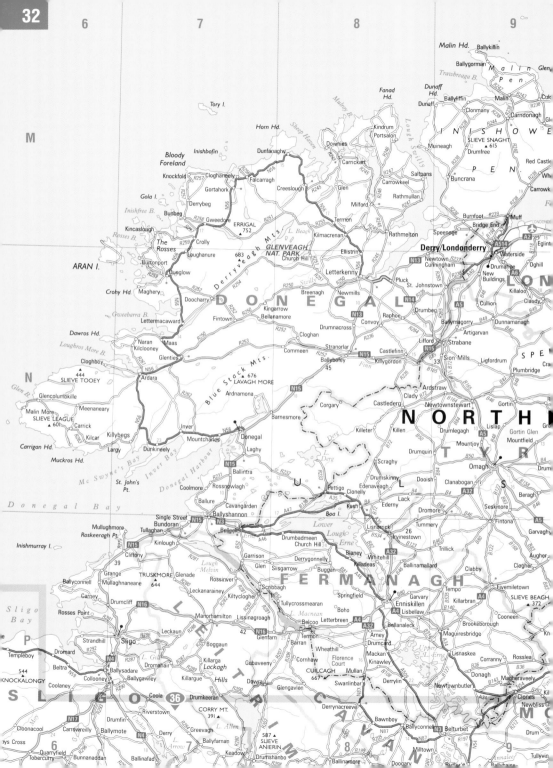

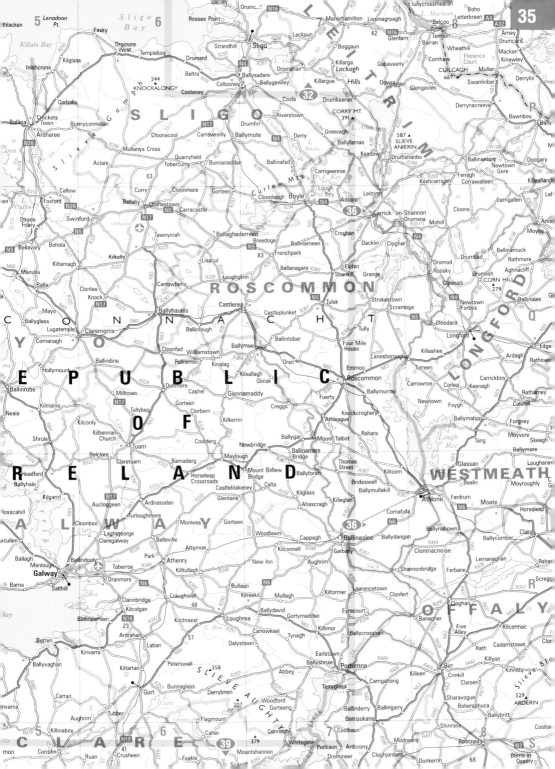

Key to Town Plan Symbols

Through Route(dual/single)	✝ Abbey/Cathedral	⛴ Historic Ship	Tourist Information Centre
Secondary Road(dual/single)	Ancient Monument	House	*i* open all year
Minor Road	Aquarium	House & Garden	*i* summer only
Pedestrian Roads	Art Gallery	Museum	Other Place of Interest
Restricted Access Roads	Bird Garden	Preserved Railway	H Hospital
Shopping Streets	Building of Public Interest	Railway Station	P Parking
Railway	Castle	Roman Antiquity	Police Station
Railway/Bus Station	Church of Interest	Theatre	Post Office
Shopping Precinct	Cinema	Tramway	Shopmobility
Park	Garden	Zoo	Youth Hostel

London

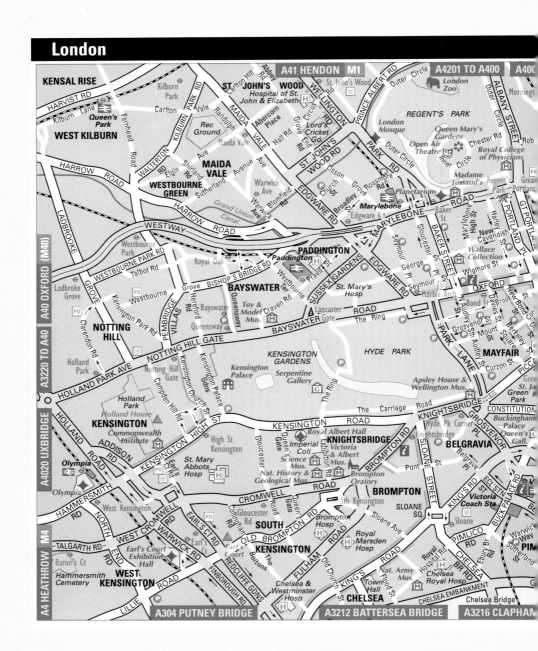

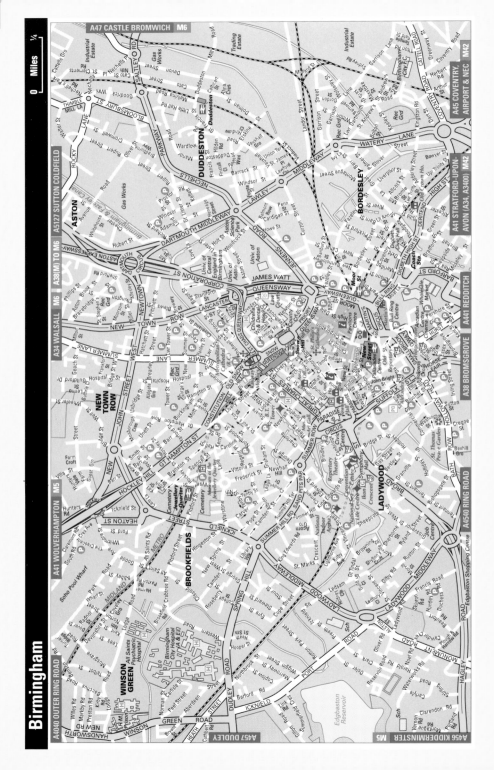

Birmingham

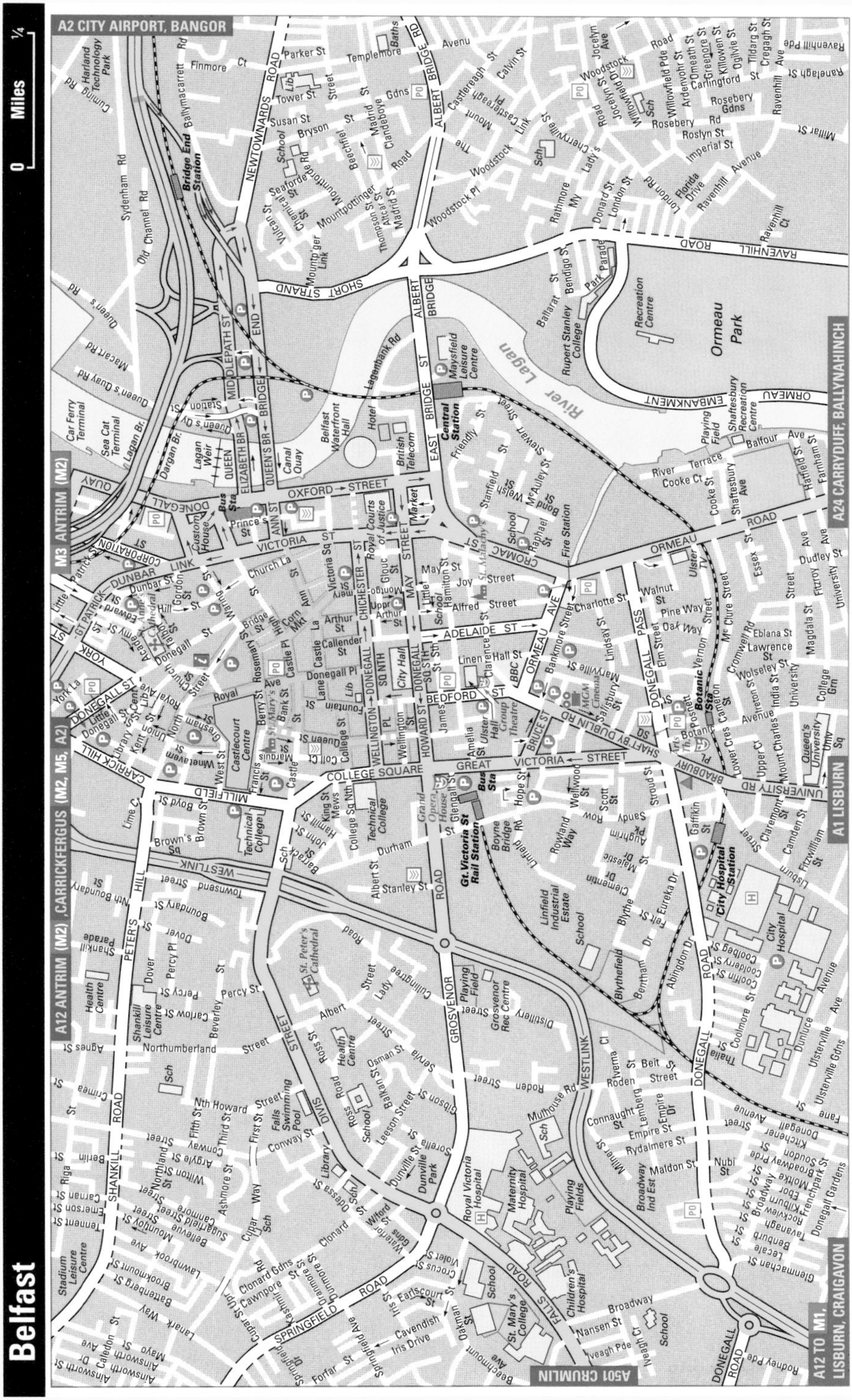

Belfast

A2 CITY AIRPORT, BANGOR

A12 ANTRIM (M2), CARRICKFERGUS (M2, M5, A2)

M3 ANTRIM (M2)

A24 CARRYDUFF, BALLYNAHINCH

A1 LISBURN

A12 TO M1, LISBURN, CRAIGAVON

A501 CRUMLIN

¼ 0 Miles

River Lagan

Ormeau Park

Central Station

Bridge End Station

Botanic Station

Gt. Victoria St Rail Station

City Hospital Station

Queen's University

City Hospital

Royal Victoria Hospital

Maternity Hospital

Children's Hospital

St Peter's Cathedral

Grand Opera House

Ulster Hall

City Hall

Waterfront Hall

Belfast Waterfront Hall

Mayfield Leisure Centre

Shaftesbury Recreation Centre

Recreation Centre

Harland Technology Park

Sea Cat Terminal

Car Ferry Terminal

Bus Sta

NEWTOWNARDS ROAD

ALBERT BRIDGE ROAD

RAVENHILL ROAD

ORMEAU ROAD

ORMEAU EMBANKMENT

OXFORD STREET

VICTORIA STREET

GREAT VICTORIA STREET

CROMAC STREET

DONEGALL PASS

UNIVERSITY RD

SHAFTESBURY SQUARE

BRADBURY

SHORT STRAND

ALBERT BRIDGE

EAST BRIDGE ST

QUEEN ELIZABETH BRIDGE

QUEEN'S BRIDGE

DONEGALL QUAY

CORPORATION ST

DUNBAR LINK

GT PATRICK ST

YORK ST

CARRICK HILL

PETER'S HILL

SHANKILL ROAD

FALLS ROAD

SPRINGFIELD ROAD

GROSVENOR ROAD

DONEGALL ROAD

WESTLINK

ADELAIDE ST

BEDFORD ST

COLLEGE SQUARE

WELLINGTON

CHICHESTER ST

ANN STREET

MAY STREET

HOWARD ST

Linfield Industrial Estate

Grosvenor Rec Centre

Dunville Park

Royal Courts

Cardiff

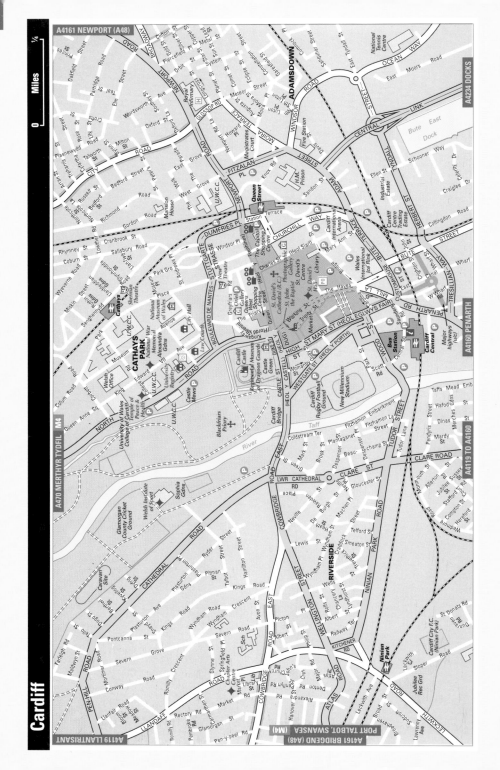

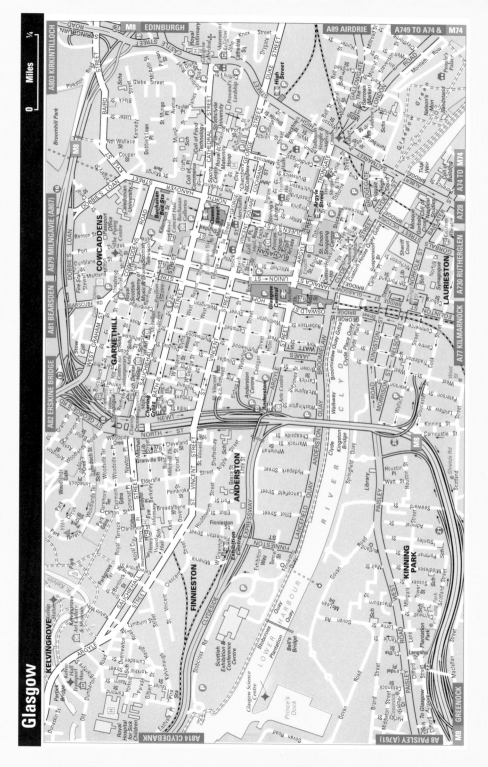

Glasgow

Dublin

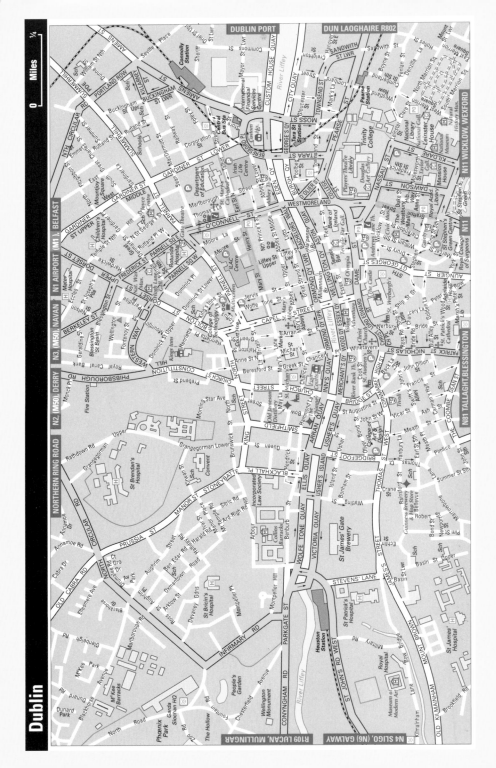

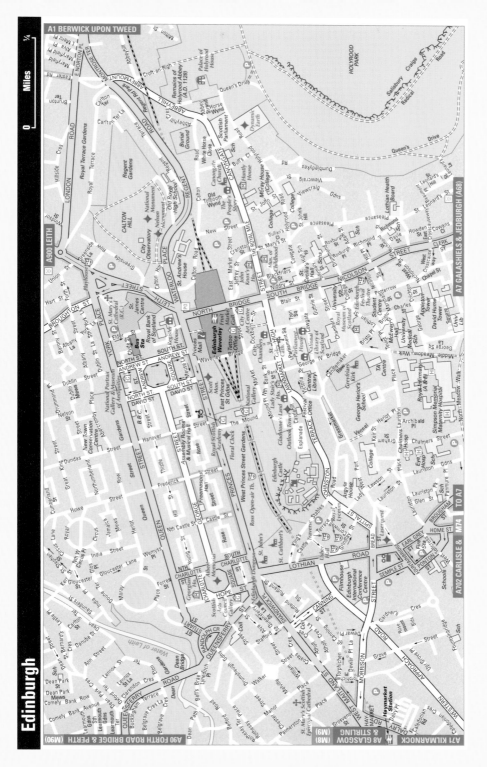

Edinburgh

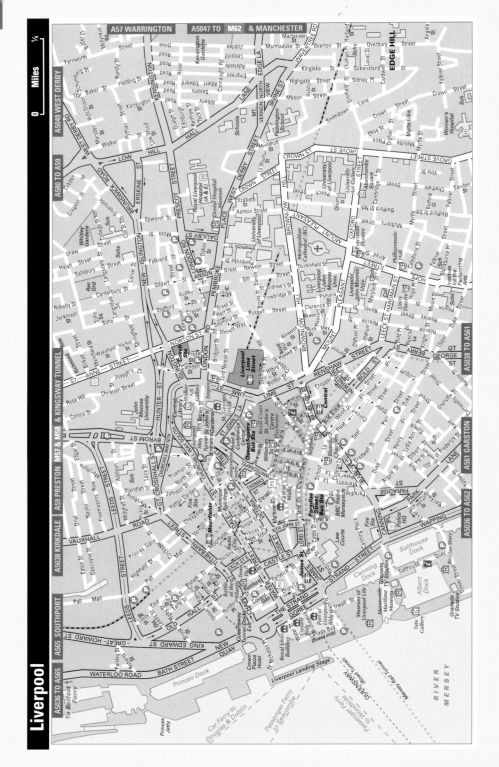

Liverpool

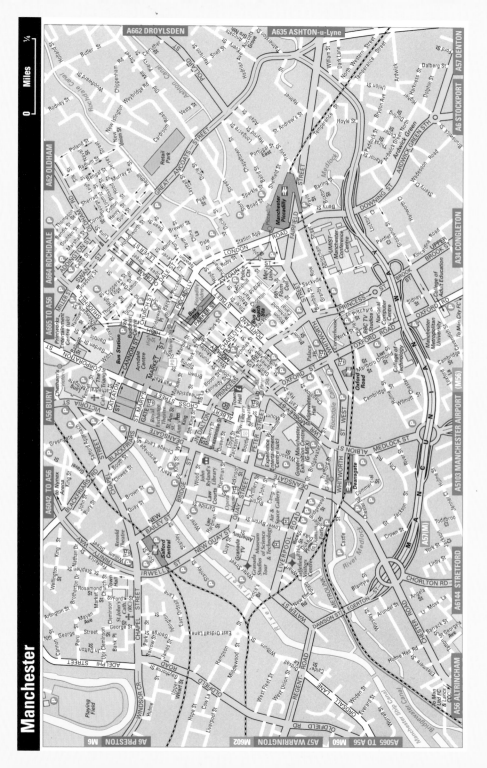

Manchester

Aberd C	Aberdeen City
Aberds	Aberdeenshire
Angl	Anglesey
Arg/Bute	Argyll & Bute
Bath/NE Som'set	Bath & North East Somerset
Beds	Bedfordshire
Bl Gwent	Blaenau Gwent
Blackb'n	Blackburn with Darwen
Blackp'l	Blackpool
Bournem'th	Bournemouth
Brackn'l	Bracknell Forest
Bridg	Bridgend
Brighton/Hove	Brighton and Hove
Bristol	City & County of Bristol
Bucks	Buckinghamshire
Caerph	Caerphilly
Cambs	Cambridgeshire
Card	Cardiff
Carms	Carmarthenshire
C/Edinb	City of Edinburgh
Ceredig'n	Ceredigion
C/Glasg	City of Glasgow
Chan Is	Channel Islands
Ches	Cheshire
Clack	Clackmannanshire
Cornw'l	Cornwall
Cumb	Cumbria
C/York	City of York
Denbs	Denbighshire
Derby	Derbyshire
Derby C	Derby City
D'lington	Darlington
Dumf/Gal	Dumfries & Galloway
Dundee C	Dundee City
E Ayrs	East Ayrshire
E Dunb	East Dunbartonshire
E Loth	East Lothian
E Renf	East Renfrewshire
ER Yorks	East Riding of Yorkshire
E Sussex	East Sussex
Falk	Falkirk
Flints	Flintshire
Glos	Gloucestershire
Gtr Lon	Greater London
Gtr Man	Greater Manchester
Gwyn	Gwynedd
Hants	Hampshire
Hartlep'l	Hartlepool
Heref'd	Herefordshire
Herts	Hertfordshire
H'land	Highland
I/Man	Isle of Man
Invercl	Inverclyde
I/Scilly	Isles of Scilly
I/Wight	Isle of Wight
Kingston/Hull	Kingston upon Hull
Lancs	Lancashire
Leics	Leicestershire
Leics C	Leicester City
Lincs	Lincolnshire
Mersey	Merseyside
Merth Tyd	Merthyr Tydfil
Middlesbro	Middlesbrough
Midloth	Midlothian
M/Keynes	Milton Keynes
Monmouths	Monmouthshire
N Ayrs	North Ayrshire
N Lanarks	North Lanarkshire
N Lincs	North Lincolnshire
N Som'set	North Somerset
N Yorks	North Yorkshire
NE Lincs	North East Lincolnshire
Neath P Talb	Neath Port Talbot
Newp	Newport
Northants	Northamptonshire
Northum	Northumberland
Nott'ham	City of Nottingham
Notts	Nottinghamshire
Oxon	Oxfordshire
Pembs	Pembrokeshire
Perth/Kinr	Perth & Kinross
Peterbro	Peterborough
Portsm'th	Portsmouth
Plym'th	Plymouth
Redcar/Clevel'd	Redcar & Cleveland
Renf	Renfrewshire
Rh Cyn Taff	Rhondda Cynon Taff
Rutl'd	Rutland
S Ayrs	South Ayrshire
S Glos	South Gloucestershire
S Lanarks	South Lanarkshire
S Yorks	South Yorkshire
Scot Borders	Scottish Borders
Shetl'd	Shetland
Shrops	Shropshire
Som'set	Somerset
Southend	Southend-on-Sea
Staffs	Staffordshire
S'thampton	Southampton
Stirl	Stirling
Stockton	Stockton on Tees
Stoke	Stoke-on-Trent
Swan	Swansea
Telford	Telford and Wrekin
Thurr'k	Thurrock
Torf	Torfaen
Tyne/Wear	Tyne & Wear
V/Glam	Vale of Glamorgan
W Berks	West Berkshire
W Dunb	West Dunbartonshire
W Isles	Western Isles
W Loth	West Lothian
W Midlands	West Midlands
W Sussex	West Sussex
W Yorks	West Yorkshire
Warwick	Warwickshire
Wilts	Wiltshire
Windsor	Windsor and Maidenhead
Worcs	Worcestershire
Wrex	Wrexham

A

Abbey *Galway* 35 R7
Abbey Town *Cumb* 20 N17
Abbeydorney *Kerry* 38 T4
Abbeyfeale *Limerick* 38 T5
Abbeyleix *Laois* 40 S9
Abbots Bromley *Staffs* 11 S20
Abbotsbury *Dorset* 4 W18
Aberaeron *Ceredig'n* 9 T15
Aberarth *Ceredig'n* 9 T15
Abercarn *Caerph* 4 U17
Aberchirder *Aberds* 29 G18
Abercrave *Powys* 9 U16
Aberdare *Rh Cyn Taff* 9 U17
Aberdaron *Gwyn* 8 S14
Aberdeen *Aberd C* 29 H19
Aberdour *Fife* 24 K17
Aberdulais *Neath P Talb* 9 U16
Aberdyfi *Gwyn* 8 S15
Aberfeldy *Perth/Kinr* 24 J16
Aberffraw *Angl* 8 S14
Aberfoyle *Stirl* 24 K15
Abergavenny *Monmouths* 4 U17
Abergele *Conwy* 8 R16
Abergwili *Carms* 9 U15
Abergwyngregyn *Gwyn* 8 R15
Abergynolwyn *Gwyn* 8 S16
Aberlady *E Loth* 25 K18
Abernethy *Perth/Kinr* 24 K17
Aberporth *Ceredig'n* 9 T14
Abersoch *Gwyn* 8 S14
Abersychan *Torf* 4 U17
Abertillery *Bl Gwent* 4 U17
Aberystwyth *Ceredig'n* 9 T15
Abingdon *Oxon* 5 U21
Abington *Limerick* 39 S7
Abington *S Lanarks* 25 H18
Aboyne *Aberds* 25 H18
Accrington *Lancs* 15 Q19
Acha *Arg/Bute* 22 J10
Achanalt *H'land* 27 G13
Achaphubuil *H'land* 23 J13
Acharacle *H'land* 23 J12
Achavanich *H'land* 28 F17
Achavraie *H'land* 27 G13
Achiemore *H'land* 27 E14
Achill *Mayo* 34 Q4
Achiltibuie *H'land* 27 F13
Achnacroish *Arg/Bute* 23 J12
Achnasheen *H'land* 27 G13
Achnashellach *H'land* 27 H13
Achosnich *H'land* 22 J11
Achriabhach *H'land* 23 J13
Acklam *N Yorks* 17 P22
Aclare *Sligo* 35 P6
Acle *Norfolk* 13 S27
Acomb *C/York* 16 Q21
Acton Burnell *Shrops* 10 S18

Acton *Armagh* 33 P11
Adamstown *Waterford* 40 T9
Adare *Limerick* 39 S6
Adcarn *Roscommon* 35 Q7
Addingham *W Yorks* 15 Q20
Adlington *Lancs* 15 Q18
Adrigole *Cork* 38 U4
Adwick le Street *S Yorks* 16 Q21
Affric Lodge *H'land* 27 H13
Aghagower *Mayo* 34 Q5
Aghalee *Antrim* 33 N11
Aghavannagh *Wicklow* 40 S11
Aghaville *Cork* 38 U5
Aghern *Cork* 39 T7
Aghnacliff *Longford* 36 Q8
Aglish *Waterford* 39 T8
Ahascragh *Galway* 35 R7
Aghoghill *Antrim* 33 N11
Ainsdale *Mersey* 15 Q17
Aird a Mhulaidh *W Isles* 26 G10
Aird Asaig Tairbeart *W Isles* 26 G10
Aird *Arg/Bute* 23 K12
Aird Uig *W Isles* 26 F9
Airdrie *N Lanarks* 19 L16
Airor *H'land* 23 H12
Airth *Falk* 24 K16
Aisgill *Cumb* 15 P19
Akeley *Bucks* 11 T22
Albrighton *Shrops* 10 S19
Alcester *Warwick* 11 T20
Aldborough *N Yorks* 16 P21
Aldbourne *Wilts* 5 V20
Aldbrough *ER Yorks* 17 Q23
Aldeburgh *Suffolk* 13 T27
Aldbury *Wilts* 5 V20
Alderley Edge *Ches* 15 R19
Aldermaston *W Berks* 5 V21
Aldershot *Hants* 6 V22
Aldridge *W Midlands* 11 S20
Aldsworth *Glos* 5 U20
Aldwick *W Sussex* 6 W22
Alexandria *W Dunb* 24 L14
Alford *Aberds* 25 H18
Alford *Lincs* 17 R24
Alfreton *Derby* 11 R21
Alfriston *E Sussex* 6 W24
Alkham *Kent* 7 V26
Allen *Kildare* 37 R10
Allendale Town *Northum* 21 N19
Allenheads *Northum* 21 N19
Allenwood *Kildare* 37 R10
Allihies *Cork* 38 U3
Alloa *Clack* 24 K16
Allonby *Cumb* 20 N17
Almondsbury *S Glos* 4 U18
Alness *H'land* 28 G15
Alnmouth *Northum* 21 M20
Alnwick *Northum* 21 M20
Alphington *Devon* 4 W16
Alrewas *Staffs* 11 S20

Alsager *Ches* 10 R19
Alston *Cumb* 21 N19
Alt na h'Airbhe *H'land* 27 G13
Altanduino *H'land* 28 F15
Altarnun *Cornw'l* 2 W14
Atlass *H'land* 28 G14
Althorne *Essex* 7 U25
Althorpe *N Lincs* 17 Q22
Altnaharra *H'land* 28 F15
Alton *Hants* 6 V22
Alton *Staffs* 11 S20
Altrincham *Gtr Man* 15 R19
Alva *Clack* 24 K16
Alvechurch *Worcs* 11 T20
Alveley *Shrops* 10 T19
Alveston *S Glos* 4 U18
Alvie *H'land* 24 H16
Alwinton *Northum* 21 M19
Alyth *Perth/Kinr* 25 J17
Amble *Northum* 21 M20
Ambleside *Cumb* 15 P18
Ambrosden *Oxon* 11 U21
Amersham *Bucks* 6 U22
Amesbury *Wilts* 5 V20
Amlwch *Angl* 8 R15
Ammanford *Carms* 9 U16
Ampleforth *N Yorks* 16 P21
Ampthill *Beds* 12 T23
Amulree *Perth/Kinr* 24 J16
An Geata Mór *Mayo* 34 P3
An t-Ob *W Isles* 26 G9
Anacotty *Limerick* 39 S6
Anascaul *Kerry* 38 T3
Ancaster *Lincs* 12 S22
Ancroft *Northum* 21 L19
Ancrum *Scot Borders* 21 L18
Andover *Hants* 5 V21
Andoversford *Glos* 11 U20
Andreas *I/Man* 14 P15
Angle *Pembs* 9 U13
Angmering *W Sussex* 6 W23
Annacarty *Tipperary* 39 S7
Annaclay *Down* 33 P12
Annagassan *Louth* 37 Q11
Annahilt *Down* 33 P12
Annalong *Down* 37 P12
Annan *Dumf/Gal* 20 N17
Annbank *S Ayrs* 19 M14
Annestown *Waterford* 40 T9
Annfield Plain *Durham* 21 N20
Anstey *Leics* 11 S21
Anstruther *Fife* 25 K18
Antrim *Antrim* 33 N11
Appleby-in-Westmorland *Cumb* 21 N19
Applecross *H'land* 27 H12
Appledore *Devon* 3 V15
Appledore *Kent* 7 V25
Araglin *Tipperary* 39 T7
Arboe *Tyrone* 33 N10
Arbroath *Angus* 25 J18
Archiestown *Moray* 28 H17
Ardagh *Limerick* 38 T5
Ardagh *Longford* 36 Q8

Ardahy *Monaghan* 33 P10
Ardara *Donegal* 32 N7
Ardarroch *H'land* 27 H12
Ardbeg *Arg/Bute* 18 L11
Ardcath *Meath* 37 Q11
Ardchyle *Stirl* 24 K15
Ardcrony *Tipperary* 36 S7
Ardee *Louth* 37 Q10
Ardentinny *Arg/Bute* 23 K14
Ardersier *H'land* 28 G15
Ardessie *H'land* 27 G13
Ardfert *Kerry* 38 T4
Ardfinnane *Tipperary* 39 T8
Ardgay *H'land* 28 G15
Ardglass *Down* 33 P12
Ardgroom *Cork* 38 U4
Ardhasig *W Isles* 26 G10
Ardingly *W Sussex* 6 V23
Ardkearagh *Kerry* 38 U3
Ardkeen *Down* 33 P12
Ardleigh *Essex* 13 U26
Ardley *Oxon* 11 U21
Ardlui *Arg/Bute* 24 K14
Ardlussa *Arg/Bute* 23 K12
Ardmore *Galway* 34 R4
Ardmore *Waterford* 39 U8
Ardnacrusha *Clare* 39 S6
Ardnamona *Donegal* 32 N7
Ardnaree *Mayo* 35 P5
Ardnasodan *Galway* 35 R6
Ardnave *Arg/Bute* 18 L11
Ardpatrick *Limerick* 39 T6
Ardrahan *Galway* 35 R6
Ardreagh *Londonderry* 33 M10
Ardrishaig *Arg/Bute* 23 K13
Ardrossan *N Ayrs* 18 L14
Ardscull *Kildare* 40 R10
Ardstraw *Tyrone* 32 N9
Ardtalnaig *Perth/Kinr* 24 J15
Ardvasar *H'land* 23 H12
Ardwell *Dumf/Gal* 18 N14
Ardwell *Moray* 29 H17
Arinagour *Arg/Bute* 22 J10
Arisaig *H'land* 23 J12
Arklow *Wicklow* 40 S11
Arless *Laois* 40 S9
Armadale *H'land* 23 H12
Armadale *W Loth* 24 L16
Armagh *Armagh* 33 P10
Armathwaite *Cumb* 20 N18
Armitage *Staffs* 11 S20
Armoy *Antrim* 33 M11
Armthorpe *S Yorks* 16 Q21
Arncliffe *N Yorks* 15 P19
Arncott *Oxon* 6 U21
Arney *Fermanagh* 32 P8
Arnisdale *H'land* 23 H12
Arnold *Notts* 11 R21
Arnside *Cumb* 15 P18
Arreton *I/Wight* 5 W21
Arrochar *Arg/Bute* 24 K14
Arthurstown *Wexford* 40 T10
Articlave *Londonderry* 33 M10
Artigarvan *Tyrone* 32 N9

Arundel *W Sussex* 6 W22
Arvagh *Cavan* 36 Q8
Ascot *Windsor* 6 V22
Asfordby *Leics* 11 S22
Ash *Kent* 7 V26
Ash *Surrey* 6 V22
Ashbourne *Meath* 37 Q11
Ashbourne *Derby* 11 R20
Ashburton *Devon* 3 W16
Ashbury *Oxon* 5 U20
Ashby de-la-Zouch *Leics* 11 S21
Ashchurch *Glos* 10 U19
Ashford *Wicklow* 40 R11
Ashford *Derby* 16 R20
Ashford *Kent* 7 V25
Ashingdon *Essex* 7 U25
Ashington *Northum* 21 M20
Ashley *Staffs* 10 S19
Ashton Keynes *Wilts* 5 U20
Ashton *Ches* 15 R18
Ashton under Hill *Worcs* 11 T20
Ashton Under Lyne *Gtr Man* 15 R19
Ashton-in-Makerfield *Gtr Man* 15 R18
Ashurst *Hants* 5 W20
Ashville *Louth* 37 Q10
Ashwater *Devon* 3 W15
Ashwell *Herts* 12 T23
Ashwick *Som'set* 4 V18
Askam-in-Furness *Cumb* 15 P17
Askeaton *Limerick* 39 S6
Askern *S Yorks* 16 Q21
Askrigg *N Yorks* 15 P19
Aslackby *Lincs* 12 S23
Aspatria *Cumb* 20 N17
Astee *Kerry* 38 S4
Astwood Bank *Worcs* 11 T20
Athboy *Meath* 37 Q10
Athea *Limerick* 38 T5
Athenry *Galway* 35 R6
Atherstone *Warwick* 11 S20
Atherton *Gtr Man* 15 R18
Athlacca *Limerick* 39 T6
Athleague *Roscommon* 35 Q7
Athlone *Westmeath* 36 R8
Athy *Kildare* 40 S10
Attical *Down* 37 P11
Attleborough *Norfolk* 13 S26
Attymon *Galway* 35 R6
Atworth *Wilts* 5 V19
Auchenblae *Aberds* 25 J19
Auchencairn *Dumf/Gal* 19 N16
Auchengray *S Lanarks* 24 L16
Auchertool *Fife* 25 K17
Auchinleck *E Ayrs* 19 M15
Auchronie *Angus* 25 J18
Auchterarder *Perth/Kinr* 24 K16
Auchterderran *Fife* 24 K17

Auchtermuchty *Fife*	25 K17		
Auchtertyre *H'land*	27 H12		
Aucloggeen *Galway*	35 R6		
Audlem *Ches*	10 S18		
Audley *Staffs*	10 R19		
Augher *Tyrone*	32 P9		
Aughnacloy *Tyrone*	33 P10		
Aughrim *Clare*	35 R6		
Aughrim *Galway*	35 R7		
Aughrim *Wicklow*	40 S11		
Auldearn *H'land*	28 G16		
Aultbea *H'land*	27 G12		
Austwick *N Yorks*	15 P19		
Avebury *Wilts*	5 V20		
Avening *Glos*	5 U19		
Aveton Gifford *Devon*	3 X16		
Aviemore *H'land*	24 H16		
Avoca *Wicklow*	40 S11		
Avoch *H'land*	28 G15		
Avonmouth *Bristol*	4 U18		
Axbridge *Som'set*	4 V18		
Axminster *Devon*	4 W17		
Axmouth *Devon*	4 W17		
Aylesbury *Bucks*	6 U22		
Aylesford *Kent*	7 V24		
Aylesham *Kent*	7 V26		
Aylsham *Norfolk*	13 S26		
Aynho *Northants*	11 U21		
Ayr *S Ayrs*	19 M14		
Aysgarth *N Yorks*	15 P19		
Ayton *N Yorks*	17 P23		
Ayton *Scot Borders*	21 L19		

B

Bac *W Isles*	26 F11		
Backwell *N Som'set*	4 V18		
Bacton *Norfolk*	13 S26		
Bacup *Lancs*	15 Q19		
Badenscoth *Aberds*	29 H19		
Badenyon *Aberds*	25 H17		
Badrallach *H'land*	27 G13		
Bagh a Chaisteil *W Isles*	22 J8		
Bagillt *Flints*	15 R17		
Bagshot *Surrey*	6 V22		
Baildon *W Yorks*	15 Q20		
Baile Ailein *W Isles*	26 F10		
Bailieborough *Cavan*	37 Q10		
Bainbridge *N Yorks*	15 P19		
Bainton *ER Yorks*	17 Q22		
Bakewell *Derby*	11 R20		
Bala *Gwyn*	8 S16		
Balbeggie *Perth/Kinr*	24 K17		
Balblair *H'land*	28 G15		
Balbriggan *Dublin*	37 Q11		
Balcombe *W Sussex*	6 V23		
Balderton *Notts*	11 R22		
Baldock *Herts*	12 U23		
Baldoyle *Dublin*	37 R11		
Balfron *Stirl*	24 K15		
Balintore *H'land*	28 G16		
Balla *Mayo*	35 Q5		
Ballachulish *H'land*	23 J13		
Ballagh *Galway*	35 R5		
Ballagh *Limerick*	38 T5		
Ballagh *Tipperary*	39 S8		
Ballaghaderreen *Roscommon*	35 Q6		
Ballantrae *S Ayrs*	18 M14		
Ballasalla *I/Man*	14 P14		
Ballater *Aberds*	25 H17		
Ballaugh *I/Man*	14 P14		
Ballickmoyler *Laois*	40 S9		
Ballin Cloher *Kerry*	38 T4		
Ballina *Mayo*	35 P5		
Ballina *Tipperary*	39 S7		
Ballinadee *Cork*	39 U6		
Ballinafad *Sligo*	35 P7		
Ballinagar *Offaly*	36 R9		
Ballinakill *Laois*	40 S9		
Ballinlack *Westmeath*	36 Q9		
Ballinlea *Wicklow*	40 R11		
Ballinalea *Longford*	36 Q8		
Ballinamallard *Fermanagh*	32 P8		
Ballinameen *Roscommon*	35 Q7		
Ballinamore Bridge *Galway*	35 R7		
Ballinamore *Leitrim*	36 P8		
Ballinascarty *Cork*	39 U6		
Ballinasloe *Galway*	35 R7		
Ballincollig *Cork*	39 U6		
Ballincurrig *Cork*	39 U7		

Ballindaggan *Wexford*	40 S10		
Ballinderreen *Galway*	35 R6		
Ballinderry *Tipperary*	35 R7		
Ballinderry Upr. *Antrim*	33 N11		
Ballindine *Mayo*	35 Q6		
Ballindooly *Galway*	35 R5		
Ballineen *Cork*	39 U6		
Ballingarry *Limerick*	39 T6		
Ballingarry *Tipperary*	36 R7		
Ballingarry *Tipperary*	39 S8		
Ballingeary *Cork*	38 U5		
Ballinhassig *Cork*	39 U6		
Ballinlea *Antrim*	33 M11		
Ballinlough *Roscommon*	35 Q6		
Ballinluig *Perth/Kinr*	24 J16		
Ballinrobe *Mayo*	35 Q5		
Ballinskelligs *Kerry*	38 U3		
Ballinspittle *Cork*	39 U6		
Ballintober *Mayo*	34 Q5		
Ballintober *Roscommon*	35 Q7		
Ballintoy *Antrim*	33 M11		
Ballintra *Donegal*	32 N7		
Ballintroohan *Donegal*	33 M9		
Ballinunty *Tipperary*	39 S8		
Ballinure *Tipperary*	39 S8		
Ballitore *Kildare*	40 R10		
Ballivor *Meath*	37 Q10		
Balloch *H'land*	28 H15		
Balloch *W Dunb*	24 K14		
Ballochan *Aberds*	25 H18		
Ballon *Carlow*	40 S10		
Ballure *Donegal*	32 N7		
Ballyagran *Limerick*	39 T6		
Ballybay *Monaghan*	37 P10		
Ballybofey *Donegal*	32 N8		
Ballyboghil *Dublin*	37 Q11		
Ballyboy *Antrim*	33 M10		
Ballybrittas *Offaly*	36 R8		
Ballybrittas *Laois*	36 R9		
Ballybrophy *Laois*	39 S8		
Ballybunion *Kerry*	38 S4		
Ballycahill *Tipperary*	39 S8		
Ballycanew *Wexford*	40 S11		
Ballycarney *Wexford*	40 S10		
Ballycarry *Antrim*	33 N12		
Ballycastle *Mayo*	34 P5		
Ballycastle *Antrim*	33 M11		
Ballyclare *Antrim*	33 N12		
Ballyclerahan *Tipperary*	39 T8		
Ballyclogh *Cork*	39 T6		
Ballycolla *Laois*	40 S9		
Ballyconneely *Galway*	34 R3		
Ballyconnell *Cavan*	36 P8		
Ballyconnell *Sligo*	32 P6		
Ballycotton *Cork*	39 U7		
Ballycrossaun *Galway*	35 R7		
Ballycroy *Mayo*	34 P4		
Ballycumber *Offaly*	36 R8		
Ballydangan *Roscommon*	36 R7		
Ballydavid *Galway*	35 R7		
Ballydavid *Kerry*	38 T3		
Ballydavis *Laois*	40 R9		
Ballydehob *Cork*	38 U5		
Ballydonegan *Cork*	38 U3		
Ballyduff *Kerry*	38 T4		
Ballyduff *Waterford*	39 T7		
Ballydugan *Down*	33 P12		
Ballyfarnan *Roscommon*	35 P7		
Ballyferriter *Kerry*	38 T3		
Ballyfin *Laois*	40 R9		
Ballyforan *Roscommon*	35 R7		
Ballygar *Galway*	35 Q7		
Ballygarrett *Wexford*	40 S11		
Ballygawley *Sligo*	32 P7		
Ballygawley *Tyrone*	33 P9		
Ballyglass *Mayo*	35 Q5		
Ballygorman *Donegal*	32 M9		
Ballygowan *Down*	33 N12		
Ballygrant *Arg/Bute*	18 L11		
Ballyhaght *Limerick*	39 T6		
Ballyhahill *Limerick*	38 S5		
Ballyhaise *Cavan*	36 P9		
Ballyhalbert *Down*	33 P13		
Ballyhale *Galway*	35 R5		
Ballyhaunis *Mayo*	35 Q6		
Ballyhean *Mayo*	35 Q5		
Ballyheige *Kerry*	38 T4		
Ballyhooly *Cork*	39 T7		

Ballyhornan *Down*	33 P12		
Ballyjamesduff *Cavan*	36 Q9		
Ballykelly *Londonderry*	33 M9		
Ballykillin *Donegal*	32 M9		
Ballylanders *Limerick*	39 T7		
Ballylaneen *Waterford*	40 T9		
Ballyliffin *Donegal*	32 M9		
Ballylongford *Kerry*	38 S5		
Ballylooby *Tipperary*	39 T8		
Ballylynan *Laois*	40 S9		
Ballymacarbry *Waterford*	39 T8		
Ballymacoda *Cork*	39 U8		
Ballymagorry *Tyrone*	32 N9		
Ballymahon *Longford*	36 Q8		
Ballymakenny *Louth*	37 Q11		
Ballymartin *Down*	37 P12		
Ballymena *Antrim*	33 N11		
Ballymoe *Galway*	35 Q7		
Ballymoney *Antrim*	33 M10		
Ballymore Eustace *Kildare*	37 R10		
Ballymore *Westmeath*	36 R8		
Ballymote *Sligo*	35 P6		
Ballymullakill *Roscommon*	36 R7		
Ballymurphy *Carlow*	40 S10		
Ballymurray *Roscommon*	36 Q7		
Ballynabola *Wexford*	40 T10		
Ballynacally *Clare*	38 S5		
Ballynacarrigy *Westmeath*	36 Q8		
Ballynacorra *Cork*	39 U7		
Ballynagore *Westmeath*	36 R9		
Ballynahinch *Down*	33 P12		
Ballynahown *Westmeath*	36 R8		
Ballynamona *Cork*	39 T6		
Ballynamult *Waterford*	39 T8		
Ballyneety *Limerick*	39 S6		
Ballynure *Antrim*	33 N12		
Ballyporeen *Tipperary*	39 T7		
Ballyragget *Kilkenny*	40 S9		
Ballyroan *Laois*	40 S9		
Ballyroe *Cork*	39 T7		
Ballyronan *Londonderry*	33 N10		
Ballyroney *Down*	33 P11		
Ballysadare *Sligo*	32 P6		
Ballyshannon *Donegal*	32 P7		
Ballyshannon *Kildare*	37 R10		
Ballyshrule *Galway*	35 R7		
Ballysloe *Tipperary*	39 S8		
Ballysteen *Limerick*	39 S6		
Ballyvaghan *Clare*	35 R5		
Ballyvourney *Cork*	38 U5		
Ballyvoy *Antrim*	33 M11		
Ballywalter *Down*	33 N13		
Ballyward *Down*	33 P11		
Ballywilliam *Wexford*	40 T10		
Balmaclellan *Dumf/Gal*	19 M15		
Balmedie *Aberds*	25 H19		
Balnapaling *H'land*	28 G15		
Balquhidder *Stirl*	24 K15		
Balrath *Meath*	37 Q11		
Balrothery *Dublin*	37 Q11		
Balsall *W Midlands*	11 T20		
Balsham *Cambs*	12 T24		
Baltimore *Cork*	39 V5		
Baltinglass *Wicklow*	40 S10		
Baltracey *Kildare*	37 R10		
Baltray *Louth*	37 Q11		
Balvicar *Arg/Bute*	23 K12		
Bamber Bridge *Lancs*	15 Q18		
Bamburgh *Northum*	21 L20		
Bamford *Derby*	16 R20		
Bampton *Devon*	4 W17		
Bampton *Oxon*	5 U20		
Banagher *Offaly*	36 R8		
Banbridge *Down*	33 P11		
Banbury *Oxon*	11 T21		
Banchory *Aberds*	25 H18		
Bandon *Cork*	39 U6		
Banff *Aberds*	29 G18		
Bangor *Mayo*	34 P4		
Bangor *Down*	33 N12		
Bangor *Gwyn*	8 R15		
Bangor-is-y-coed *Wrex*	10 S18		

Banham *Norfolk*	13 T26		
Bankend *Dumf/Gal*	20 M16		
Bankfoot *Perth/Kinr*	24 J16		
Bankhead *Aberd C*	25 H19		
Banks *Lancs*	15 Q18		
Bannockburn *Stirl*	24 K16		
Bannow *Wexford*	40 T10		
Banstead *Surrey*	6 V23		
Banteer *Cork*	39 T6		
Bantry *Cork*	38 U5		
Banwell *N Som'set*	4 V18		
Bar Hill *Cambs*	12 T24		
Barabhas *W Isles*	26 F10		
Baranailt *Londonderry*	33 N9		
Barassie *S Ayrs*	19 L14		
Barbon *Cumb*	15 P18		
Bardney *Lincs*	17 R23		
Barefield *Clare*	35 S6		
Barford *Warwick*	11 T20		
Bargoed *Caerph*	4 U17		
Bargrennan *Dumf/Gal*	19 M14		
Barham *Kent*	7 V26		
Barkway *Herts*	12 U24		
Barlborough *Derby*	16 R21		
Barlby *N Yorks*	16 Q21		
Barley *Herts*	12 T24		
Barmby Moor *ER Yorks*	17 Q22		
Barmoor Castle *Northum*	21 L19		
Barmouth *Gwyn*	8 S15		
Barna *Galway*	35 R5		
Barnaderg *Galway*	35 R6		
Barnard Castle *Durham*	21 N20		
Barnesmore *Donegal*	32 N7		
Barnet *Gtr Lon*	6 U23		
Barnetby le Wold *N Lincs*	17 Q23		
Barnham *Suffolk*	13 T25		
Barnhill *Moray*	28 G17		
Barnoldswick *Lancs*	15 Q19		
Barnsley *S Yorks*	16 Q21		
Barnstaple *Devon*	3 V15		
Barnt Green *Worcs*	11 T20		
Barr *S Ayrs*	19 M14		
Barraduff *Kerry*	38 T5		
Barran *Cavan*	32 P8		
Barrhead *E Renf*	19 L15		
Barrhill *S Ayrs*	18 M14		
Barrow upon Humber *N Lincs*	17 Q23		
Barrowford *Lancs*	15 Q19		
Barrow-in-Furness *Cumb*	15 P17		
Barry *Angus*	25 K18		
Barry *V/Glam*	4 V17		
Barton *N Yorks*	16 P20		
Barton upon Humber *N Lincs*	17 Q23		
Barton-le-Clay *Beds*	6 U22		
Barwell *Leics*	11 S21		
Baschurch *Shrops*	10 S18		
Basildon *Essex*	7 U25		
Basingstoke *Hants*	5 V21		
Baslow *Derby*	16 R20		
Baston *Lincs*	12 S23		
Bath *Bath/NE Som'set*	5 V19		
Bathford *Bath/NE Som'set*	5 V19		
Bathgate *W Loth*	24 L16		
Batley *W Yorks*	16 Q20		
Battersown *Meath*	37 R10		
Battle *E Sussex*	7 W24		
Bawdeswell *Norfolk*	13 S26		
Bawdsey *Suffolk*	13 T26		
Bawnboy *Cavan*	36 P8		
Bawtry *S Yorks*	16 R21		
Bayston Hill *Shrops*	10 S18		
Beachley *Glos*	4 U18		
Beaconsfield *Bucks*	6 U22		
Beadnell *Northum*	21 L20		
Bealin *Westmeath*	36 R8		
Bealnablath *Cork*	39 U6		
Beaminster *Dorset*	4 W18		
Bearsden *E Dunb*	19 L15		
Bearsted *Kent*	7 V25		
Beattock *Dumf/Gal*	20 M17		
Beaufort *Kerry*	38 T4		
Beaufort *Bl Gwent*	4 U17		
Beaulieu *Hants*	5 W21		
Beauly *H'land*	28 H15		
Beaumaris *Angl*	8 R15		
Bebington *Mersey*	15 R17		
Beccles *Suffolk*	13 T27		
Beck Row *Suffolk*	12 T24		

Beckermet *Cumb*	14 P16		
Beckfoot *Cumb*	20 N17		
Beckhampton *Wilts*	5 V20		
Beckingham *Notts*	17 R22		
Beckington *Som'set*	5 V19		
Bedale *N Yorks*	16 P20		
Beddgelert *Gwyn*	8 R15		
Bedford *Beds*	12 T23		
Bedlington *Northum*	21 M20		
Bedwas *Caerph*	4 U17		
Bedworth *Warwick*	11 T21		
Beech Hill *Down*	33 P11		
Beeford *ER Yorks*	17 Q23		
Beelaha *Clare*	38 S4		
Beer *Devon*	4 W17		
Beeston *Notts*	11 S21		
Beeswing *Dumf/Gal*	19 M16		
Begelly *Pembs*	9 U14		
Beguildy *Powys*	10 T17		
Beighton *S Yorks*	16 R21		
Beith *N Ayrs*	19 L14		
Belbroughton *Worcs*	10 T19		
Belchford *Lincs*	17 R23		
Belclare *Galway*	35 R6		
Belcoo *Fermanagh*	32 P8		
Belderg *Mayo*	34 P4		
Belfast *Antrim*	33 N12		
Belford *Northum*	21 L20		
Belgooly *Cork*	39 U7		
Bellacorick *Mayo*	34 P4		
Bellaghy *Londonderry*	33 N10		
Bellahy *Sligo*	35 Q6		
Bellanagare *Roscommon*	35 Q7		
Bellanaleck *Fermanagh*	32 P8		
Bellanamore *Donegal*	32 N7		
Bellananagh *Cavan*	36 Q9		
Bellavary *Mayo*	35 Q5		
Belleek *Donegal*	32 P7		
Belleek *Armagh*	33 P11		
Belleville *Galway*	35 R6		
Bellinamuck *Longford*	36 Q8		
Bellingham *Northum*	21 M19		
Bellsbank *E Ayrs*	19 M15		
Bellshill *N Lanarks*	19 L15		
Belmont *Blackb'n*	15 Q19		
Belmullet *Mayo*	34 P4		
Belper *Derby*	11 R21		
Belsay *Northum*	21 M20		
Beltinge *Kent*	7 V26		
Belton *N Lincs*	17 Q22		
Belton *Norfolk*	13 S27		
Beltra *Mayo*	34 Q5		
Beltra *Sligo*	32 P6		
Belturbet *Cavan*	36 P9		
Bembridge *I/Wight*	5 W21		
Benburb *Tyrone*	33 P10		
Benington *Lincs*	12 R24		
Benllech *Angl*	8 R15		
Bennettsbridge *Kilkenny*	40 S9		
Benson *Oxon*	5 U21		
Bentley *Hants*	6 V22		
Bentley *S Yorks*	16 Q21		
Benwick *Cambs*	12 T23		
Beragh *Tyrone*	32 N9		
Bere Alston *Devon*	3 X15		
Bere Regis *Dorset*	5 W19		
Berkeley *Glos*	5 U19		
Berkhamsted *Herts*	6 U22		
Berriedale *H'land*	28 F17		
Berriew *Powys*	10 S17		
Berrow *Som'set*	4 V17		
Berwick *E Sussex*	6 W24		
Berwick-Upon-Tweed *Northum*	21 L19		
Bessbrook *Armagh*	33 P11		
Bethersden *Kent*	7 V25		
Bethesda *Gwyn*	8 R15		
Bettws Bledrws *Ceredig'n*	9 T15		
Bettyhill *H'land*	28 E15		
Bettystown *Meath*	37 Q11		
Betws *Bridg*	9 U16		
Betws-y-Coed *Conwy*	8 R16		
Beulah *Powys*	9 T16		
Beverley *ER Yorks*	17 Q23		
Beville *Mayo*	34 P5		
Bewcastle *Cumb*	21 M18		
Bewdley *Worcs*	10 T19		
Bexhill *E Sussex*	7 W24		
Bexley *Gtr Lon*	6 V24		
Bibury *Glos*	5 U20		
Bicester *Oxon*	11 U21		
Bickington *Devon*	4 W16		

Bicton *Shrops* 10 S18
Biddenden *Kent* 7 V25
Biddulph *Staffs* 10 R19
Bideford *Devon* 3 V15
Bidford-on-Avon
 Warwick 11 T20
Bigbury *Devon* 3 X16
Biggar *S Lanarks* 20 L16
Biggin Hill *Gtr Lon* 6 V24
Biggleswade *Beds* 12 T23
Bildeston *Suffolk* 13 T25
Billericay *Essex* 7 U24
Billesdon *Leics* 11 S21
Billingborough *Lincs* 12 S23
Billingham *Stockton* 21 N21
Billinghay *Lincs* 12 R23
Billingshurst
 W Sussex 6 V23
Bilston *W Midlands* 10 S19
Binbrook *Lincs* 17 R23
Bingham *Notts* 11 S22
Bingley *W Yorks* 15 Q20
Birchgrove *Swan* 9 U16
Birchington *Kent* 7 V26
Birdhill *Tipperary* 39 S7
Birdlip *Glos* 5 U19
Birkdale *Mersey* 15 Q17
Birkenhead *Mersey* 15 R17
Birmingham
 W Midlands 11 T20
Birr *Offaly* 36 R8
Birtley *Northum* 21 M19
Birtley *Tyne/Wear* 21 N20
Bishop Auckland
 Durham 21 N20
Bishop Monkton
 N Yorks 16 P21
Bishopbriggs *E Dunb* 19 L15
Bishop's Castle
 Shrops 10 T18
Bishop's Cleeve *Glos* 10 U19
Bishop's Frome
 Heref'd 10 T19
Bishops Lydeard
 Som'set 4 V17
Bishop's Nympton
 Devon 3 W16
Bishop's Stortford
 Herts 6 U24
Bishop's Tawton
 Devon 3 V15
Bishop's Waltham
 Hants 5 W21
Bishopsteignton
 Devon 4 W16
Bishopstoke *Hants* 5 W21
Bishopston *Swan* 9 U15
Bitton *S Glos* 5 V19
Blaby *Leics* 11 S21
Black Rock *Louth* 37 Q11
Blackburn *Blackb'n* 15 Q19
Blackford *Cumb* 20 N17
Blackford *Perth/Kinr* 24 K16
Blackpool *Blackp'l* 15 Q17
Blackridge *W Loth* 19 L16
Blackrock *Dublin* 37 R11
Blackwater *Wexford* 40 T11
Blackwaterfoot
 N Ayrs 18 L13
Blackwood *Caerph* 4 U17
Blackwood
 S Lanarks 19 L16
Blaenau Ffestiniog
 Gwyn 8 S16
Blaenavon *Torf* 4 U17
Blagdon *N Som'set* 4 V18
Blaina *Bl Gwent* 4 U17
Blair Atholl *Perth/Kinr* 24 J16
Blairgowrie
 Perth/Kinr 24 J17
Blakeney *Glos* 5 U19
Blakeney *Norfolk* 13 S26
Blanchland *Northum* 21 N19
Blanchardstown
 Dublin 37 R11
Blandford Forum
 Dorset 5 W19
Blaney *Fermanagh* 32 P8
Blarney *Cork* 39 U6
Blaydon *Tyne/Wear* 21 N20
Bleadon *N Som'set* 4 V18
Blean *Kent* 7 V26
Blessington *Wicklow* 37 R10
Bletchingdon *Oxon* 5 U21
Bletchley *M/Keynes* 12 U22
Blewbury *Oxon* 5 U21
Blidworth *Notts* 11 R22
Blisworth *Northants* 11 T22
Blockley *Glos* 11 T20

Blofield *Norfolk* 13 S26
Bloxham *Oxon* 11 T21
Blubberhouses
 N Yorks 16 Q20
Blundeston *Norfolk* 13 S27
Blyth Bridge
 Scot Borders 20 L17
Blyth *Northum* 21 M20
Blyth *Notts* 16 R21
Blythburgh *Suffolk* 13 T27
Blythe Bridge *Staffs* 10 S19
Blyton *Lincs* 17 R22
Boat of Garten
 H'land 24 H16
Boddam *Aberds* 29 H20
Bodedern *Angl* 8 R14
Bodenham *Heref'd* 10 T18
Bodiam *E Sussex* 7 V25
Bodinnick *Cornw'l* 2 X14
Bodmin *Cornw'l* 2 X14
Bodyke *Clare* 39 S6
Boggaun *Leitrim* 32 P7
Bognor Regis
 W Sussex 6 W22
Boheraphuca *Offaly* 36 R8
Boherboy *Cork* 38 T5
Boherlahan *Tipperary* 39 S8
Boho *Fermanagh* 32 P8
Bohola *Mayo* 35 Q5
Boldon *Tyne/Wear* 21 N21
Bolea *Londonderry* 33 M10
Boley *Kildare* 40 R10
Bollington *Ches* 15 R19
Bolney *W Sussex* 6 W23
Bolsover *Derby* 16 R21
Bolton Abbey
 N Yorks 15 Q20
Bolton Bridge
 N Yorks 15 Q20
Bolton by Bowland
 Lancs 15 Q19
Bolton le Sands
 Lancs 15 P18
Bolton Gtr Man 15 Q19
Bonarbridge *H'land* 28 G15
Bonby *N Lincs* 17 Q23
Bonchester Bridge
 Scot Borders 21 M18
Bonchurch *I/Wight* 5 W21
Bo'ness *Falk* 24 K16
Bonhill *W Dunb* 24 L14
Bonnybridge *Falk* 24 K16
Bonnyrigg *Midloth* 20 L17
Bonvilston *V/Glam* 4 V17
Boot *Cumb* 15 P17
Bootle *Cumb* 14 P17
Bootle *Mersey* 15 R17
Bordon *Hants* 6 V22
Borehamwood *Herts* 6 U23
Boreland *Dumf/Gal* 20 M17
Borgh *W Isles* 26 F11
Borgue *Dumf/Gal* 19 N15
Borough Green *Kent* 7 V24
Boroughbridge
 N Yorks 16 P21
Borris *Carlow* 40 S10
Borris-in-Ossory
 Laois 36 S8
Borrisokane
 Tipperary 36 S7
Borrisoleigh
 Tipperary 39 S8
Borrowdale *Cumb* 15 N17
Borth *Ceredig'n* 8 T15
Bosbury *Heref'd* 10 T19
Boscastle *Cornw'l* 2 W14
Bosham *W Sussex* 6 W22
Boston Spa *W Yorks* 16 Q21
Boston *Lincs* 12 S23
Botesdale *Suffolk* 13 T25
Bothel *Cumb* 20 N17
Bothenhampton
 Dorset 4 W18
Botley *Oxon* 5 U21
Bottesford *Leics* 11 S22
Bottisham *Cambs* 12 T24
Botwnnog *Gwyn* 8 S14
Bouladuff *Tipperary* 39 S8
Bourne End *Bucks* 6 U22
Bourne *Lincs* 12 S23
Bournemouth
 Bournem'th 5 W20
Bourton-on-the-
 Water *Glos* 11 U20
Bovey Tracey *Devon* 4 W16
Bow *Devon* 3 W16
Bowes *Durham* 15 N20
Bowmore *Arg/Bute* 18 L11
Bowness-on-Solway
 Cumb 20 N17

Bowness-on-
 Windermere *Cumb* 15 P18
Box *Wilts* 5 V19
Boyle *Roscommon* 35 Q7
Bozeat *Northants* 12 T22
Brabourne Lees *Kent* 7 V25
Brabourne *Kent* 7 V25
Bracadale *H'land* 26 H11
Bracebridge Heath
 Lincs 12 R23
Bracklesham
 W Sussex 6 W22
Brackley *Northants* 11 T21
Bracklin *Cavan* 37 Q10
Bracknagh *Offaly* 36 R9
Bracknell *Brackn'l* 6 V22
Braco *Perth/Kinr* 24 K16
Bradford on Avon
 Wilts 5 V19
Bradford *W Yorks* 15 Q20
Brading *I/Wight* 5 W21
Bradpole *Dorset* 4 W18
Bradwell-on-Sea
 Essex 7 U25
Bradworthy *Devon* 3 W15
Brae Roy Lodge
 H'land 24 J14
Braemar *Aberds* 24 H17
Braemore *H'land* 27 G13
Braemore *H'land* 28 F16
Brailsford *Derby* 11 S20
Braintree *Essex* 7 U25
Bramford *Suffolk* 13 T26
Bramhall *Gtr Man* 15 R19
Bramhope *W Yorks* 16 Q20
Brampton *Cambs* 12 T23
Brampton *Cumb* 21 N18
Brancaster *Norfolk* 13 S25
Branden *Kerry* 38 T3
Branderburgh *Moray* 28 G17
Brandon *Durham* 21 N20
Brandon *Suffolk* 13 T25
Branston *Lincs* 17 R23
Brantham *Suffolk* 13 U26
Bratton Fleming
 Devon 3 V16
Braunston *Northants* 11 T21
Braunton *Devon* 3 V15
Bray *Wicklow* 37 R11
Bray *Windsor* 6 U22
Breage *Cornw'l* 2 X13
Breaghva *Clare* 38 S4
Breakish *H'land* 23 H12
Bream *Glos* 4 U18
Breanais *W Isles* 26 F9
Brechfa *Carms* 9 U15
Brechin *Angus* 25 J18
Brecon *Powys* 9 U17
Brede *E Sussex* 7 W25
Bredenbury *Heref'd* 10 T18
Breedoge
 Roscommon 35 Q7
Breenagh *Donegal* 32 N8
Brent *Gtr Lon* 6 U23
Brentwood *Essex* 7 U24
Bretforton *Worcs* 11 T20
Brewood *Staffs* 10 S19
Bride *I/Man* 14 P15
Bridestowe *Devon* 3 W15
Brideswell
 Roscommon 36 R7
Bridge End *Donegal* 32 M9
Bridge of Allan *Stirl* 24 K16
Bridge of Balgie
 Perth/Kinr 24 J15
Bridge of Cally
 Perth/Kinr 24 J17
Bridge of Don
 Aberd C 25 H19
Bridge of Earn
 Perth/Kinr 24 K17
Bridge of Orchy
 Arg/Bute 24 J14
Bridge of Weir *Renf* 19 L14
Bridge *Kent* 7 V26
Bridgend *Arg/Bute* 18 L11
Bridgend *Bridg* 4 U16
Bridgetown *Wexford* 40 T10
Bridgnorth *Shrops* 10 S19
Bridgwater *Som'set* 4 V18
Bridlington *ER Yorks* 17 P23
Bridport *Dorset* 4 W18
Brierfield *Lancs* 15 Q19
Brierley Hill
 W Midlands 10 T19
Brigg *N Lincs* 17 Q23
Brighouse *W Yorks* 15 Q20
Brighstone *I/Wight* 5 W21
Brightlingsea *Essex* 7 U26

Brighton
 Brighton/Hove 6 W23
Brigstock *Northants* 12 T22
Brill *Bucks* 6 U21
Brimfield *Heref'd* 10 T18
Brinklow *Warwick* 11 T21
Brinkworth *Wilts* 5 U20
Bristol *Bristol* 4 V18
Briston *Norfolk* 13 S26
Briton Ferry
 Neath P Talb 9 U16
Brittas *Dublin* 37 R11
Brixham *Torbay* 3 X16
Brixton *Devon* 3 X15
Brixworth *Northants* 11 T22
Brize Norton *Oxon* 5 U20
Broad Chalke *Wilts* 5 V20
Broad Haven *Pembs* 9 U13
Broad Hinton *Wilts* 5 V20
Broadclyst *Devon* 4 W17
Broadford *Clare* 39 S6
Broadford *Limerick* 39 T6
Broadford *H'land* 23 H12
Broadhembury
 Devon 4 W17
Broadmayne *Dorset* 5 W19
Broadstairs *Kent* 7 V26
Broadstone *Poole* 5 W19
Broadwas *Worcs* 10 T19
Broadway *Wexford* 40 T11
Broadway *Worcs* 11 T20
Broadwey *Dorset* 5 W19
Broadwindsor *Dorset* 4 W18
Brochel *H'land* 27 H11
Brockenhurst *Hants* 5 W20
Brockworth *Glos* 5 U19
Brocton *Staffs* 10 S19
Brodick *N Ayrs* 18 L13
Bromfield *Shrops* 10 T18
Bromham *Beds* 12 T22
Bromham *Wilts* 5 V19
Bromley Green *Kent* 7 V25
Bromley *Gtr Lon* 6 V24
Brompton Regis
 Som'set 4 V16
Brompton *N Yorks* 16 P21
Bromsgrove *Worcs* 10 T19
Bromyard *Heref'd* 10 T19
Brooke *Norfolk* 13 S26
Brookeborough
 Fermanagh 32 P9
Broomfield
 Monaghan 37 P10
Broomfield *Essex* 7 U24
Broomhaugh
 Northum 21 N20
Broomhill *Northum* 21 M20
Brora *H'land* 28 F16
Broseley *Shrops* 10 S19
Brothertoft *Lincs* 12 S23
Brotton
 Redcar/Clevel'd 17 N22
Brough *Cumb* 15 N19
Brough *ER Yorks* 17 Q22
Brough *H'land* 28 E17
Broughderg *Tyrone* 33 N10
Broughshane *Antrim* 33 N11
Broughton Astley
 Leics 11 S21
Broughton *Cumb* 20 N17
Broughton *Hants* 5 V20
Broughton *Lancs* 15 Q18
Broughton *N Lincs* 17 Q22
Broughton *Northants* 11 T22
Broughton
 Scot Borders 20 L17
Broughton-in-
 Furness *Cumb* 15 P17
Broughty Ferry
 Dundee C 25 K18
Brownhills
 W Midlands 11 S20
Broxburn *W Loth* 24 L17
Broxton *Ches* 10 R18
Bruff *Limerick* 39 T6
Bruichladdich
 Arg/Bute 18 L11
Brundall *Norfolk* 13 S26
Brunton *Northum* 21 L20
Brunton *Northum* 21 M19
Bruree *Limerick* 39 T6
Bruton *Som'set* 5 V19
Brymbo *Wrex* 10 R17
Brynamman *Carms* 9 U16
Bryncrug *Gwyn* 8 S15
Brynmawr *Bl Gwent* 4 U17
Brynsiencyn *Angl* 8 R15
Bubwith *ER Yorks* 17 Q22
Buchlyvie *Stirl* 24 K15

Buckden *Cambs* 12 T23
Buckden *N Yorks* 15 P19
Buckfast *Devon* 3 X16
Buckfastleigh *Devon* 3 X16
Buckhaven *Fife* 25 K17
Buckie *Moray* 29 G18
Buckingham *Bucks* 11 T22
Buckland Brewer
 Devon 3 W15
Buckland Newton
 Dorset 5 W19
Buckland *Oxon* 5 U21
Buckley *Flints* 10 R17
Buck's Cross *Devon* 3 W15
Bucksburn *Aberd C* 25 H19
Bude *Cornw'l* 2 W14
Budleigh Salterton
 Devon 4 W17
Bugbrooke *Northants* 11 T22
Buggan *Fermanagh* 32 P8
Bugle *Cornw'l* 2 X14
Builth Wells *Powys* 9 T17
Bulford *Wilts* 5 V20
Bulkington *Warwick* 11 T21
Bullaun *Galway* 35 R6
Bulwell *Nott'ham* 11 R21
Bunahowen *Mayo* 34 P4
Bunalunn *Cork* 38 U5
Bunaw *Kerry* 38 U4
Bunbeg *Donegal* 32 M7
Bunbrosna
 Westmeath 36 Q9
Bunbury *Ches* 10 R18
Bunclody *Wexford* 40 S10
Buncrana *Donegal* 32 M9
Bundoran *Donegal* 32 P7
Bunessan *Arg/Bute* 22 K11
Bungay *Suffolk* 13 T26
Bunmahon *Waterford* 40 T9
Bunnaglass *Galway* 35 R6
Bunnahabhain
 Arg/Bute 18 L11
Bunnanaddan *Sligo* 35 P6
Bunnyconnellan
 Mayo 35 P5
Bunratty *Clare* 39 S6
Buntingford *Herts* 12 U23
Bunwell *Norfolk* 13 S26
Burbage *Derby* 15 R20
Burbage *Leics* 11 S21
Burbage *Wilts* 5 V20
Bures *Suffolk* 13 U25
Burford *Oxon* 5 U20
Burgess Hill
 W Sussex 6 W23
Burgh le Marsh *Lincs* 12 R24
Burgh-by-Sands
 Cumb 20 N17
Burghclere *Hants* 5 V21
Burghead *Moray* 28 G17
Burghfield Common
 W Berks 6 V21
Burley *Hants* 5 W20
Burley *W Yorks* 15 Q20
Burlton *Shrops* 10 S18
Burneside *Cumb* 15 P18
Burnfoot *Cork* 39 T6
Burnfoot *Donegal* 32 M9
Burnham Market
 Norfolk 13 S25
Burnham *Bucks* 6 U22
Burnham-on-Crouch
 Essex 7 U25
Burnham-on-Sea
 Som'set 4 V18
Burniston *N Yorks* 17 P23
Burnley *Lancs* 15 Q19
Burnmouth
 Scot Borders 21 L19
Burntisland *Fife* 25 K17
Burntwood *Staffs* 11 S20
Burrelton *Perth/Kinr* 24 J17
Burren *Clare* 35 R5
Burren Down 37 P11
Burry Port *Carms* 9 U15
Burscough Bridge
 Lancs 15 Q18
Burstwick *ER Yorks* 17 Q23
Burton Agnes
 ER Yorks 17 P23
Burton Bradstock
 Dorset 4 W18
Burton Fleming
 ER Yorks 17 P23
Burton in Lonsdale
 N Yorks 15 P18
Burton Latimer
 Northants 12 T22
Burton *Cumb* 15 P18

Burton upon Stather *N Lincs* 17 Q22
Burton Upon Trent *Staffs* 11 S20
Burtonport *Donegal* 32 N7
Burwash *E Sussex* 7 W24
Burwell *Cambs* 12 T24
Bury St. Edmunds *Suffolk* 12 T24
Bury *Gtr Man* 15 Q19
Bushey *Herts* 6 U23
Bushmills *Antrim* 33 M10
Butler's Bridge *Cavan* 36 P9
Butlerstown *Cork* 39 U6
Buttermere *Cumb* 20 N17
Buttevant *Cork* 39 T6
Buxted *E Sussex* 6 W24
Buxton *Derby* 15 R20
Bweeng *Cork* 39 T6
Byfield *Northants* 11 T21
Byfleet *Surrey* 6 V23
Bylchau *Conwy* 8 R16

C

Cabinteely *Dublin* 37 R11
Cabrach *Moray* 29 H17
Cabragh *Tyrone* 33 P10
Cadamstown *Offaly* 36 R8
Caenby Corner *Lincs* 17 R22
Caergwrle *Flints* 10 R17
Caerleon *Newp* 4 U18
Caernarfon *Gwyn* 8 R15
Caerphilly *Caerph* 4 U17
Caersws *Powys* 8 S17
Caerwent *Monmouths* 4 U18
Caher *Clare* 35 S6
Caher *Galway* 34 R5
Caher *Tipperary* 39 T8
Caherciveen *Kerry* 38 U3
Caherconlish *Limerick* 39 S7
Caherdaniel *Kerry* 38 U3
Cahermore *Cork* 38 U3
Cahermurphy *Clare* 38 S5
Cairinis *W Isles* 26 G9
Cairndow *Arg/Bute* 23 K14
Cairnryan *Dumf/Gal* 18 N13
Caister-on-Sea *Norfolk* 13 S27
Caistor *Lincs* 17 R23
Calanais *W Isles* 26 F10
Caldbeck *Cumb* 20 N17
Calder Bridge *Cumb* 14 P17
Caldercruix *N Lanarks* 19 L16
Caldicot *Monmouths* 4 U18
Caledon *Tyrone* 33 P10
Calgary *Arg/Bute* 22 J11
Callan *Kilkenny* 40 S9
Callander *Stirl* 24 K15
Callington *Cornw'l* 3 X15
Callow *Galway* 34 R3
Callow *Mayo* 35 Q5
Calne *Wilts* 5 V20
Calshot *Hants* 5 W21
Calstock *Cornw'l* 3 X15
Calta *Galway* 35 R7
Calverton *Notts* 11 R21
Cam *Glos* 5 U19
Camber *E Sussex* 7 W25
Camberley *Surrey* 6 V22
Cambo *Northum* 21 M20
Camborne *Cornw'l* 2 X13
Cambridge *Cambs* 12 T24
Camden *Gtr Lon* 6 U23
Camelford *Cornw'l* 2 W14
Camlough *Armagh* 33 P11
Cammachmore *Aberds* 25 H19
Camolin *Wexford* 40 S11
Camp *Kerry* 38 T4
Campbeltown *Arg/Bute* 18 M12
Campile *Wexford* 40 T10
Camrose *Pembs* 9 U13
Camross *Wexford* 40 T10
Canisbay *H'land* 29 E17
Cannich *H'land* 27 H14
Canningstown *Cavan* 36 Q9
Cannington *Som'set* 4 V17
Cannock *Staffs* 10 S19
Canonbie *Dumf/Gal* 20 M18
Canterbury *Kent* 7 V26

Canvey *Essex* 7 U25
Caol *H'land* 23 J13
Caolas Stocinis *W Isles* 26 G10
Caoles *Arg/Bute* 22 J10
Capel Curig *Conwy* 8 R16
Capel St. Mary *Suffolk* 13 T26
Capel *Surrey* 6 V23
Cappagh *Cork* 39 T7
Cappagh *Galway* 35 R7
Cappagh White *Tipperary* 39 S7
Cappamore *Limerick* 39 S7
Cappeen *Cork* 39 U6
Cappoquin *Waterford* 39 T8
Carbis Bay *Cornw'l* 2 X13
Carbost *H'land* 26 H11
Carbost *H'land* 26 H11
Carbury *Kildare* 37 R10
Cardiff *Card* 4 V17
Cardigan *Ceredig'n* 9 T14
Cardington *Beds* 12 T23
Cardross *Arg/Bute* 19 L14
Cargill *Perth/Kinr* 24 J17
Carhampton *Som'set* 4 V17
Carisbrooke *I/Wight* 5 W21
Cark *Cumb* 15 P18
Carlabhagh *W Isles* 26 F10
Carlanstown *Meath* 37 Q10
Carleton Rode *Norfolk* 13 S26
Carlingford *Louth* 37 P11
Carlisle *Cumb* 20 N18
Carlops *Scot Borders* 19 L17
Carlow *Carlow* 40 S10
Carlton Colville *Suffolk* 13 T27
Carlton Miniott *N Yorks* 16 P21
Carlton *N Yorks* 16 Q21
Carlton *Notts* 11 S21
Carlton-in-Lindrick *Notts* 16 R21
Carluke *S Lanarks* 19 L16
Carmarthen *Carms* 9 U15
Carmyllie *Angus* 25 J18
Carna *H'land* 22 J12
Carnachuin *H'land* 24 H16
Carnaross *Meath* 37 Q10
Carncastle *Antrim* 33 N12
Carndonagh *Donegal* 32 M9
Carnew *Wicklow* 40 S11
Carney *Sligo* 32 P6
Carnforth *Lancs* 15 P18
Carnlough *Antrim* 33 N12
Carno *Powys* 8 S16
Carnoustie *Angus* 25 J18
Carnwath *S Lanarks* 20 L16
Carracastle *Mayo* 35 Q6
Carradale *Arg/Bute* 18 L13
Carragh *Kildare* 37 R10
Carraroe *Galway* 34 R4
Carrbridge *H'land* 28 H16
Carrick *Donegal* 32 N6
Carrick *Arg/Bute* 23 K14
Carrickart *Donegal* 32 M8
Carrickbeg *Waterford* 40 T9
Carrickboy *Longford* 36 Q8
Carrickfergus *Antrim* 33 N12
Carrickmacross *Monaghan* 37 Q10
Carrickmore *Tyrone* 33 N9
Carrick-on-Shannon *Roscommon* 36 Q7
Carrick-on-Suir *Tipperary* 40 T9
Carrigaholt *Clare* 38 S4
Carrigahorig *Tipperary* 36 R7
Carrigaline *Cork* 39 U7
Carrigallen *Leitrim* 36 Q8
Carriganimmy *Cork* 38 U5
Carrigfada *Cork* 38 U5
Carrigkerry *Limerick* 38 T5
Carrignavar *Cork* 39 U7
Carrigtohill *Cork* 39 U7
Carronbridge *Dumf/Gal* 19 M16
Carrowbehy *Roscommon* 35 Q6
Carrowkeel *Donegal* 32 M9
Carrowkeel *Donegal* 32 M9
Carrowkeel *Galway* 35 R7
Carrowkennedy *Mayo* 34 Q4
Carrowreagh *Antrim* 33 M11
Carrowreilly *Sligo* 35 P6

Carrowroe *Longford* 36 Q8
Carryduff *Down* 33 N12
Carsaig *Arg/Bute* 23 K12
Carsphairn *Dumf/Gal* 19 M15
Carstairs *S Lanarks* 20 L16
Carterton *Oxon* 5 U20
Cartmel *Cumb* 15 P18
Cashel *Galway* 35 Q6
Cashel *Tipperary* 39 S8
Castle Acre *Norfolk* 13 S25
Castle Cary *Som'set* 4 V18
Castle Donington *Leics* 11 S21
Castle Douglas *Dumf/Gal* 19 N16
Castlebar *Mayo* 34 Q5
Castlebellingham *Louth* 37 Q11
Castleblakeney *Galway* 35 R7
Castleblaney *Monaghan* 37 P10
Castlebridge *Wexford* 40 T11
Castlecomer *Kilkenny* 40 S9
Castleconnell *Limerick* 39 S7
Castlecor *Cork* 39 T6
Castledawson *Londonderry* 33 N10
Castlederg *Tyrone* 32 N8
Castledermot *Kildare* 40 S10
Castlefinn *Donegal* 32 N8
Castleford *W Yorks* 16 Q21
Castlegregory *Kerry* 38 T3
Castlehill *Mayo* 34 P4
Castleisland *Kerry* 38 T5
Castlelyons *Cork* 39 T7
Castlemaine *Kerry* 38 T4
Castlemartin *Pembs* 9 U13
Castlemartyr *Cork* 39 U7
Castleplunket *Roscommon* 35 Q7
Castlepollard *Westmeath* 36 Q9
Castlerea *Roscommon* 35 Q7
Castlerock *Londonderry* 33 M10
Castleside *Durham* 21 N20
Castleton *Derby* 15 R20
Castleton *N Yorks* 17 P22
Castletown Bearhaven *Cork* 38 U4
Castletown Geoghegan *Westmeath* 36 R9
Castletown *Laois* 36 S9
Castletown *Meath* 37 Q10
Castletown *I/Man* 14 P14
Castletownroche *Cork* 39 T7
Castletownshend *Cork* 38 U5
Castlewellan *Down* 33 P12
Caston *Norfolk* 13 S25
Castor *Peterbro* 12 S23
Catcleugh *Northum* 21 M19
Caterham *Surrey* 6 V23
Caton *Lancs* 15 P18
Catrine *E Ayrs* 19 L15
Catsfield *E Sussex* 7 W24
Catterall *Lancs* 15 Q18
Catterick Camp *N Yorks* 16 P20
Catterick *N Yorks* 16 P20
Catton *Northum* 21 N19
Caulkerbush *Dumf/Gal* 20 N16
Causeway *Kerry* 38 T4
Cavan *Cavan* 36 Q9
Cavangarden *Donegal* 32 N7
Cawdor *H'land* 28 G16
Cawood *N Yorks* 16 Q21
Cawston *Norfolk* 13 S26
Caythorpe *Lincs* 12 R22
Cefn-mawr *Wrex* 10 S17
Celbridge *Kildare* 37 R10
Cemaes *Angl* 8 R15
Cemmaes Road *Powys* 8 S16
Cenarth *Carms* 9 T14
Ceres *Fife* 25 K18
Cerne Abbas *Dorset* 5 W19
Cerrigydrudion *Conwy* 8 R16
Chacewater *Cornw'l* 2 X13

Chaddesley Corbet *Worcs* 10 T19
Chadwell St. Mary *Thurr'k* 7 V24
Chagford *Devon* 3 W16
Chalfont St. Giles *Bucks* 6 U22
Chalford *Glos* 5 U19
Chalgrove *Oxon* 6 U21
Challacombe *Devon* 3 V16
Challock *Kent* 7 V25
Chandler's Ford *Hants* 5 W21
Chanonrock *Louth* 37 Q10
Chapel en le Frith *Derby* 15 R20
Chapel St. Leonards *Lincs* 17 R24
Chapeltown *S Lanarks* 19 L15
Chapeltown *S Yorks* 16 R21
Chard *Som'set* 4 W18
Charing *Kent* 7 V25
Charlbury *Oxon* 11 U21
Charlemont *Armagh* 33 P10
Charlestown *Mayo* 35 Q6
Charlestown of Aberlour *Moray* 29 H17
Charleville *Cork* 39 T6
Charlton Horethorne *Som'set* 5 W19
Charlton Kings *Glos* 10 U19
Charlton *Wilts* 5 U19
Charlwood *Surrey* 6 V23
Charminster *Dorset* 5 W19
Charmouth *Dorset* 4 W18
Chartham *Kent* 7 V26
Chasel *Mayo* 34 Q4
Chathill *Northum* 21 L20
Chatteris *Cambs* 12 T24
Chatton *Northum* 21 L20
Chawleigh *Devon* 3 W16
Cheadle *Gtr Man* 15 R19
Cheadle *Staffs* 11 S20
Chedburgh *Suffolk* 13 T25
Cheddar *Som'set* 4 V18
Cheddleton *Staffs* 10 R19
Chellaston *Derby C* 11 S21
Chelmarsh *Shrops* 10 T19
Chelmsford *Essex* 7 U24
Cheltenham *Glos* 10 U19
Chepstow *Monmouths* 4 U18
Cherhill *Wilts* 5 V20
Cheriton Fitzpaine *Devon* 4 W16
Cheriton *Hants* 5 V21
Chertsey *Surrey* 6 V22
Chesham *Bucks* 6 U22
Cheshunt *Herts* 6 U23
Chester *Ches* 10 R18
Chesterfield *Derby* 16 R21
Chester-le-Street *Durham* 21 N20
Chew Magna *Bath/NE Som'set* 4 V18
Chewton Mendip *Som'set* 4 V18
Chichester *W Sussex* 6 W22
Chiddingfold *Surrey* 6 V22
Chideock *Dorset* 4 W18
Chigwell *Essex* 6 U24
Chilcompton *Som'set* 4 V18
Chilham *Kent* 7 V25
Chillington *Devon* 3 X16
Chilton *Durham* 21 N20
Chingford *Gtr Lon* 6 U24
Chinnor *Oxon* 6 U22
Chippenham *Wilts* 5 V19
Chipping Campden *Glos* 11 T20
Chipping Norton *Oxon* 11 U20
Chipping Ongar *Essex* 7 U24
Chipping Sodbury *S Glos* 5 U19
Chirbury *Shrops* 10 S17
Chirk *Wrex* 10 S17
Chirnside *Scot Borders* 21 L19
Chiselborough *Swindon* 5 U20
Chitterne *Wilts* 5 V19
Chobham *Surrey* 6 V22
Chollerton *Northum* 21 M19
Cholsey *Oxon* 5 U21
Chorley *Lancs* 15 Q18
Chorleywood *Herts* 6 U22

Christchurch *Cambs* 12 S24
Christchurch *Dorset* 5 W20
Christow *Devon* 4 W16
Chudleigh *Devon* 4 W16
Chulmleigh *Devon* 3 W16
Church Hill *Donegal* 32 N8
Church Hill *Fermanagh* 32 P8
Church Stretton *Shrops* 10 S18
Church Village *Rh Cyn Taff* 9 U17
Churchdown *Glos* 10 U19
Churchill *Oxon* 11 U20
Churchstow *Devon* 3 X16
Churchtown *Cork* 39 U7
Churchtown *Wexford* 40 T11
Chwilog *Gwyn* 8 S15
Cilgerran *Pembs* 9 T14
Cille Bhrighde *W Isles* 22 H9
Cilycwm *Carms* 9 T16
Cinderford *Glos* 5 U19
Cirencester *Glos* 5 U20
Clabby *Fermanagh* 32 P9
Clabhach *Arg/Bute* 22 J10
Clachan na Luib *W Isles* 26 G9
Clachan *Arg/Bute* 18 L12
Clachan *H'land* 27 H11
Clackmannan *Clack* 24 K16
Clacton-on-Sea *Essex* 7 U26
Cladich *Arg/Bute* 23 K13
Clady Milltown *Armagh* 33 P10
Clady *Tyrone* 32 N8
Claggan *H'land* 23 J12
Claigan *H'land* 26 H10
Clanabogan *Tyrone* 32 N9
Clane *Kildare* 37 R10
Clanfield *Hants* 6 W22
Claonaig *Arg/Bute* 18 L13
Clapham *Beds* 12 T23
Clapham *N Yorks* 15 P19
Clara *Offaly* 36 R8
Clarahill *Laois* 36 R9
Clare *Suffolk* 13 T25
Clarecastle *Clare* 39 S6
Clareen *Offaly* 36 R8
Claregalway *Galway* 35 R6
Claremorris *Mayo* 35 Q5
Claretuam *Galway* 35 R6
Clarina *Limerick* 39 S6
Clarinbridge *Galway* 35 R6
Clash *Cork* 39 U7
Clashmore *Waterford* 39 T8
Clashmore *H'land* 28 G15
Claudy *Londonderry* 32 N9
Clavering *Essex* 12 U24
Claverley *Shrops* 10 S19
Clawton *Devon* 3 W15
Clay Cross *Derby* 11 R21
Claydon *Suffolk* 13 T26
Claypole *Lincs* 12 R22
Cleadale *H'land* 22 J11
Cleady *Kerry* 38 U4
Cleator Moor *Cumb* 14 N16
Cleethorpes *NE Lincs* 17 Q23
Cleeve Prior *Warwick* 11 T20
Cleggan *Galway* 34 Q3
Clehonger *Heref'd* 10 T18
Cleobury Mortimer *Shrops* 10 T19
Clevedon *N Som'set* 4 V18
Cleveleys *Lancs* 15 Q17
Cley *Norfolk* 13 S26
Clifden *Galway* 34 R3
Cliffe *Medway* 7 V25
Cliffony *Sligo* 32 P7
Clifford *Heref'd* 10 T17
Clipston *Northants* 11 T22
Clitheroe *Lancs* 15 Q19
Clive *Shrops* 10 S18
Clogh *Kilkenny* 40 S9
Clogh *Antrim* 33 N11
Cloghan *Donegal* 32 N8
Cloghan *Offaly* 36 R8
Cloghan *Westmeath* 36 Q9
Cloghane *Kerry* 38 T3
Cloghaneely *Donegal* 32 M7
Cloghboy *Donegal* 32 N6
Clogheen *Tipperary* 39 T8
Clogher Head *Louth* 37 Q11
Clogher *Roscommon* 35 Q7
Clogher *Tyrone* 32 P9
Cloghjordan *Tipperary* 36 S7
Cloghran *Dublin* 37 R11

Cloghy Down 33 P13
Clomantagh Kilkenny 40 S9
Clonakilty Cork 39 U6
Clonaslee Laois 36 R8
Clonbulloge Offaly 36 R9
Clonbur Galway 34 Q5
Cloncurry Kildare 37 R10
Clondalkin Dublin 37 R11
Clonea Waterford 40 T9
Clonee Meath 37 R11
Cloneen Tipperary 39 T8
Clonelly Fermanagh 32 N8
Clones Monaghan 32 P9
Cloney Kildare 40 R8
Clonfert Galway 36 R7
Clonlee Mayo 35 Q6
Clonmacnoise Offaly 36 R8
Clonmany Donegal 32 M9
Clonmel Tipperary 39 T8
Clonmellon
  Westmeath 36 Q9
Clonmore Carlow 40 S10
Clonmore Offaly 36 R9
Clonmore Tipperary 39 S8
Clonord Meath 36 R9
Clonroche Wexford 40 T10
Clontarf Dublin 37 R11
Cloodara Longford 36 Q8
Cloonacool Sligo 35 P6
Cloonart Longford 36 Q8
Cloonbannin Cork 38 T5
Cloonboo Galway 35 R5
Cloone Leitrim 36 Q8
Cloonfad
  Roscommon 35 Q6
Cloonkeen Kerry 38 U5
Cloonlara Clare 39 S6
Cloonloogh Sligo 35 Q7
Cloonmore Mayo 35 Q6
Clophill Beds 12 T23
Clorbern Galway 35 Q6
Closeburn Dumf/Gal 19 M16
Clough Down 33 P12
Cloughton N Yorks 17 P23
Clova Angus 25 J17
Clovelly Devon 3 W15
Clovenfords
  Scot Borders 20 L18
Clowne Derby 16 R21
Cloyne Cork 39 U7
Clun Shrops 10 T17
Clunbury Shrops 10 T17
Clunes H'land 23 J14
Clungunford Shrops 10 T17
Clutton
  Bath/NE Som'set 4 V18
Clydach Swan 9 U16
Clydebank W Dunb 19 L15
Clynnog-fawr Gwyn 8 R15
Clyro Powys 10 T17
Coachford Cork 39 U6
Cóbh Cork 39 U7
Coagh Tyrone 33 N10
Coalbrookdale
  Telford 10 S18
Coalburn S Lanarks 19 L16
Coalisland Tyrone 33 N10
Coalville Leics 11 S21
Coatbridge
  N Lanarks 19 L15
Cobham Kent 7 V24
Cobham Surrey 6 V23
Cock Bridge Aberds 25 H17
Cockburnspath
  Scot Borders 25 L19
Cockenzie E Loth 25 L19
Cockerham Lancs 15 Q18
Cockermouth Cumb 20 N17
Cockfield Durham 21 N20
Cockfield Suffolk 13 T25
Cockshutt Shrops 10 S18
Coddenham Suffolk 13 T26
Codford St. Mary
  Wilts 5 V19
Coggeshall Essex 7 U25
Coignafearn Lodge
  H'land 24 H15
Coille Mhorgil H'land 23 H13
Coillore H'land 26 H11
Colby I/Man 14 P14
Colchester Essex 13 U25
Cold Ashton S Glos 5 V19
Coldingham
  Scot Borders 21 L19
Coldstream
  Scot Borders 21 L19
Colebrooke Devon 4 W16
Coleford Glos 4 U18
Colehill Longford 36 Q8

Coleraine
  Londonderry 33 M10
Coleshill Warwick 11 T20
Colinton C/Edinb 25 L17
Colintraive Arg/Bute 18 L13
Collin Dumf/Gal 20 M16
Collingbourne
  Kingston Wilts 5 V20
Collingham Notts 11 R22
Collingham W Yorks 16 Q21
Collinstown
  Westmeath 36 Q9
Collon Louth 37 Q11
Collooney Sligo 32 P7
Colmonel S Ayrs 18 M14
Colne Lancs 15 Q19
Colpy Aberds 29 H18
Colsterworth Lincs 12 S22
Coltishall Norfolk 13 S26
Colwell Northum 21 M19
Colwich Staffs 11 S20
Colwyn Bay Conwy 8 R16
Colyton Devon 4 W17
Combe Martin Devon 3 V15
Comber Down 33 N12
Comberton Cambs 12 T24
Combwich Som'set 4 V17
Commeen Donegal 32 N8
Compton Martin
  Bath/NE Som'set 4 V18
Compton W Berks 5 U21
Compton W Sussex 6 W22
Comrie Perth/Kinr 24 K16
Condover Shrops 10 S18
Cong Mayo 34 Q5
Congleton Ches 10 R19
Congresbury
  N Som'set 4 V18
Coningsby Lincs 12 R23
Conisbrough S Yorks 16 R21
Coniston Cumb 15 P17
Conlig Down 33 N12
Conna Cork 39 T7
Connagh Galway 35 S7
Connah's Quay Flints 15 R17
Connel Park N Ayrs 19 M15
Connel Arg/Bute 23 K13
Connonagh Cork 38 U5
Connor Antrim 33 N11
Cononbridge H'land 28 G15
Consett Durham 21 N20
Contin H'land 28 G14
Convoy Donegal 32 N8
Conwy Conwy 8 R16
Cookham Windsor 6 U22
Cookstown Tyrone 33 N10
Coola Sligo 35 P7
Coolaney Sligo 32 P6
Coolbaun Tipperary 35 S7
Coolderg Galway 35 Q6
Coole Westmeath 36 Q9
Coolgreany Wexford 40 S11
Coolham W Sussex 6 W23
Coolmore Donegal 32 N7
Coolrain Laois 36 S8
Coombe Bissett Wilts 5 V19
Cooneen Fermanagh 32 P9
Cooraclare Clare 38 S5
Cootehill Cavan 36 P9
Copplestone Devon 4 W16
Coppull Lancs 15 Q18
Copthorne W Sussex 6 V23
Corbally Laois 40 S9
Corbally Sligo 35 P5
Corbridge Northum 21 N19
Corby Glen Lincs 12 S22
Corby Northants 12 T22
Cordal Kerry 38 T5
Corfe Castle Dorset 5 W19
Corfe Mullen Dorset 5 W19
Corgary Tyrone 32 N8
Cork Cork 39 U7
Corlea Longford 36 Q8
Corlogh Mayo 34 P3
Cornafulla
  Roscommon 36 R8
Cornamona Galway 34 Q5
Cornanagh Mayo 35 Q5
Cornhaw Cavan 32 P8
Cornhill on Tweed
  Northum 21 L19
Corpach H'land 23 J13
Corran H'land 23 J13
Corranny Fermanagh 32 P9
Corrawalleen Leitrim 36 P8
Corrie N Ayrs 18 L13
Corrigeenroe
  Roscommon 35 P7
Corringham Lincs 17 R22
Corringham Thurr'k 7 U25

Corris Gwyn 8 S16
Corrofin Clare 35 S5
Corsham Wilts 5 V19
Corsley Wilts 5 V19
Corsock Dumf/Gal 19 M16
Corton Norfolk 13 S27
Corvally Monaghan 37 Q10
Corvoy Monaghan 37 Q10
Corwen Denbs 8 S19
Coseley W Midlands 10 S19
Cosham Portsm'th 6 W21
Costelloe Galway 34 R4
Costessey Norfolk 13 S26
Cotgrave Notts 11 S21
Cotherstone Durham 21 N20
Cottenham Cambs 12 T24
Cottered Herts 12 U23
Cottesmore Rutl'd 12 S22
Cottingham ER Yorks 17 Q23
Coulags H'land 27 H13
Coulport Arg/Bute 23 K14
Countesthorpe Leics 11 S21
Coupar Angus
  Perth/Kinr 24 J17
Courtmacsherry Cork 39 U6
Courtown Wexford 40 S11
Cove Bay Aberd C 25 H19
Cove Arg/Bute 23 L14
Cove H'land 27 G12
Coventry W Midlands 11 T21
Coverack Cornw'l 2 X13
Cowbit Lincs 12 S23
Cowbridge V/Glam 4 V17
Cowdenbeath Fife 24 K17
Cowes I/Wight 5 W21
Cowfold W Sussex 6 W23
Cowpen Northum 21 M20
Complain Hants 6 W21
Coxheath Kent 7 V25
Coylton S Ayrs 19 M14
Craanford Wexford 40 S11
Craggie H'land 28 H15
Crai Powys 9 U16
Craibstone Moray 29 G18
Craigavon Armagh 33 P11
Craigellachie Moray 29 H17
Craighouse Arg/Bute 18 L12
Craigmore Arg/Bute 18 L13
Craignure Arg/Bute 23 K12
Craigtown H'land 28 F16
Crail Fife 25 K18
Cramlington Northum 21 M20
Cranagh Tyrone 33 N9
Cranborne Dorset 5 W20
Cranbrook Kent 7 V25
Cranleigh Surrey 6 V23
Cranmore Som'set 5 V19
Cranwell Lincs 12 R23
Cratloe Limerick 38 T5
Crathie Aberds 25 H17
Craughwell Galway 35 R6
Craven Arms Shrops 10 T18
Crawford S Lanarks 20 M16
Crawfordjohn
  S Lanarks 19 L16
Crawley W Sussex 6 V23
Creag Ghoraidh
  W Isles 26 H9
Creaghanroe
  Monaghan 33 P10
Creake Norfolk 13 S25
Credenhill Heref'd 10 T18
Crediton Devon 4 W16
Creegh Clare 38 S5
Creeragh Mayo 35 P5
Creeslough Donegal 32 M8
Creetown Dumf/Gal 19 N15
Creeve Tyrone 33 N10
Creeves Limerick 38 S5
Creggan Tyrone 33 N9
Cregganbaun Mayo 34 Q4
Creggs Galway 35 Q7
Cressage Shrops 10 S18
Cresselly Pembs 9 U14
Crewe Ches 10 R19
Crewkerne Som'set 4 W18
Crianlarich Stirl 24 K14
Criccieth Gwyn 8 S15
Crick Northants 11 T21
Crickhowell Powys 4 U17
Cricklade Wilts 5 U20
Crieff Perth/Kinr 24 K16
Crimond Aberds 29 G20
Crinan Arg/Bute 23 K12
Crindle Londonderry 33 M10
Crinkill Offaly 36 R8
Croagh Limerick 39 S6
Crocketford
  Dumf/Gal 19 M16
Crockets Town Mayo 35 P5

Croggan Arg/Bute 23 K12
Croghan Offaly 36 R9
Croghan
  Roscommon 35 Q7
Croglin Cumb 21 N18
Croick H'land 28 G14
Crolly Donegal 32 M7
Cromarty H'land 28 G15
Cromer Norfolk 13 S26
Cromor W Isles 26 F11
Crondall Hants 6 V22
Crook Durham 21 N20
Crookedwood
  Westmeath 36 Q9
Crookham Northum 21 L19
Crookhaven Cork 39 V4
Crooklands Cumb 15 P18
Crookstown Cork 39 U6
Croom Limerick 39 S6
Crosbost W Isles 26 F11
Crosby Ravensworth
  Cumb 21 N18
Crosby Cumb 20 N17
Crosby Mersey 15 R17
Cross Barry Cork 39 U6
Cross Keys Meath 37 Q10
Crossakiel Meath 36 Q9
Crossdoney Cavan 36 Q9
Crossgar Down 33 P12
Cross-Hands Carms 9 U15
Crosshaven Cork 39 U7
Crosshill S Ayrs 19 M14
Crossmaglen Armagh 37 P10
Crossmichael
  Dumf/Gal 19 N16
Crossmolina Mayo 34 P5
Croston Lancs 15 Q18
Crowborough
  E Sussex 6 V24
Crowland Lincs 12 S23
Crowle N Lincs 17 Q22
Crowthorne
  Wokingham 6 V22
Croxton Kerrial Leics 11 S22
Croyde Devon 3 V15
Croydon Gtr Lon 6 V23
Cruden Bay Aberds 29 H20
Crudgington Telford 10 S18
Crumlin Dublin 37 R11
Crumlin Antrim 33 N11
Crusheen Clare 35 S6
Crymych Pembs 9 U14
Cuckfield W Sussex 6 V23
Cuddington Bucks 6 U22
Cuddington Ches 15 R18
Cudworth S Yorks 16 Q21
Cuffley Herts 6 U23
Culdaff Donegal 32 M9
Culgaith Cumb 21 N18
Culkein H'land 27 F13
Cullaville Armagh 37 P10
Cullen Tipperary 39 S7
Cullen Moray 29 G18
Cullicudden H'land 28 G15
Cullinane Antrim 33 N11
Cullion Tyrone 32 N9
Culloden H'land 28 H15
Cullompton Devon 4 W17
Cullyhanna Armagh 37 P10
Culmaize Dumf/Gal 19 N15
Culmington Shrops 10 T18
Culmstock Devon 4 W17
Culrain H'land 28 G15
Culross Fife 24 K16
Cults Aberd C 25 H19
Cumbernauld
  N Lanarks 19 L16
Cuminestown Aberds 29 G19
Cummertrees
  Dumf/Gal 20 N17
Cumnock E Ayrs 19 M15
Cumnor Oxon 5 U21
Cumwhinton Cumb 20 N18
Cupar Fife 25 K17
Curraglass Cork 39 T7
Currie C/Edinb 24 L17
Curry Sligo 35 Q6
Curry Rivel Som'set 4 V18
Curryglass Cork 38 U4
Cushendall Antrim 33 M11
Cushendun Antrim 33 M11
Cushina Offaly 36 R9
Cwmafan
  Neath P Talb 9 U16
Cwmann Carms 9 T15
Cwmbran Torf 4 U17
Cwrt Gwyn 8 S16
Cymmer
  Neath P Talb 9 U16
Cynwyl Elfed Carms 9 U15

D
Dacklin Roscommon 36 Q7
Dagenham Gtr Lon 6 U24
Dail bho Dheas
  W Isles 26 F11
Dailly S Ayrs 19 M14
Daingean Offaly 36 R9
Dalabrog W Isles 22 H9
Dalbeattie Dumf/Gal 19 N16
Dale Pembs 9 U13
Dalguise Perth/Kinr 24 J16
Dalhalvaig H'land 28 F16
Dalkeith Midloth 25 L17
Dalkey Dublin 37 R11
Dallas Moray 28 G17
Dalleagles E Ayrs 19 M15
Dalmally Arg/Bute 23 K14
Dalmellington E Ayrs 19 M15
Dalnaspidal
  Perth/Kinr 24 J15
Dalnessie H'land 28 F15
Dalry Dumf/Gal 19 M15
Dalry N Ayrs 19 L14
Dalrymple E Ayrs 19 M14
Dalston Cumb 20 N18
Dalton Dumf/Gal 20 M17
Dalton N Yorks 16 P20
Dalton-in-Furness
  Cumb 15 P17
Dalwhinnie H'land 24 J15
Dalystown Galway 35 R7
Damerham Hants 5 W20
Damerstown Kilkenny 40 S9
Danbury Essex 7 U25
Darkley Armagh 33 P10
Darlington D'lington 16 N20
Darragh Clare 38 S5
Dartford Kent 6 V24
Dartington Devon 3 X16
Dartmouth Devon 3 X16
Darton S Yorks 16 Q20
Darvel E Ayrs 19 L15
Darwen Blackb'n 15 Q19
Daventry Northants 11 T21
Davington Dumf/Gal 20 M17
Dawlish Devon 4 W17
Deal Kent 7 V26
Dearham Cumb 20 N17
Dearne S Yorks 16 Q21
Debenham Suffolk 13 T26
Deddington Oxon 11 U21
Deelish Cork 38 U5
Deeping St. Nicholas
  Lincs 12 S23
Deganwy Conwy 8 R16
Delabole Cornw'l 2 W14
Delchirach Moray 28 H17
Delves Durham 21 N20
Delvin Westmeath 36 Q9
Denbigh Denbs 8 R17
Denby Dale W Yorks 16 Q20
Denholm
  Scot Borders 21 M18
Denny Falk 24 K16
Dent Cumb 15 P19
Denton Gtr Man 15 R19
Denton Lincs 12 S22
Derby Derby C 11 S21
Derry Sligo 35 P7
Derry/Londonderry
  Londonderry 32 N9
Derrybeg Donegal 32 M7
Derryboy Down 33 P12
Derrybrien Galway 35 R6
Derrycoosh Mayo 34 Q5
Derrygonnelly
  Fermanagh 32 P8
Derrygorry
  Monaghan 33 P9
Derrygrogan Offaly 36 R9
Derrykeighan Antrim 33 M10
Derrylin Fermanagh 32 P8
Derrymore Kerry 38 T4
Derrynacreeve Cavan 36 P8
Derrynane Kerry 38 U3
Derryrush Galway 34 R4
Derrytrasna Armagh 33 N11
Dersingham Norfolk 13 S25
Dervaig Arg/Bute 22 J11
Dervock Antrim 33 M11
Desborough
  Northants 11 T22
Desertmartin
  Londonderry 33 N10
Desford Leics 11 S21
Devil's Bridge
  Ceredig'n 9 T16

Devizes *Wilts* 5 V20
Devonport *Plym'th* 3 X15
Dewsbury *W Yorks* 16 Q20
Diabaig *H'land* 27 G12
Diamond *Down* 33 P11
Dibden Purlieu *Hants* 5 W21
Dickleborough
  Norfolk 13 T26
Didcot *Oxon* 5 U21
Digby *Lincs* 12 R23
Dinas Mawddwy
  Gwyn 8 S16
Dinas Powis *V/Glam* 4 V17
Dingle *Kerry* 38 T3
Dingwall *H'land* 28 G15
Dinnington *S Yorks* 16 R21
Dinton *Wilts* 5 V20
Dippen *N Ayrs* 18 M13
Dirleton *E Loth* 25 K18
Dirtagh *Londonderry* 33 M10
Diss *Norfolk* 13 T26
Distington *Cumb* 20 N16
Ditchingham *Norfolk* 13 T26
Ditchling *E Sussex* 6 W23
Dittisham *Devon* 3 X16
Ditton Priors *Shrops* 10 T18
Doagh *Antrim* 33 N11
Dobwalls *Cornw'l* 2 X14
Docking *Norfolk* 13 S25
Dockray *Cumb* 20 N18
Doddinghurst *Essex* 7 U24
Doddington *Cambs* 12 S24
Doddington *Northum* 21 L19
Dolanog *Powys* 8 S17
Dolfor *Powys* 8 T17
Dolgarrog *Conwy* 8 R16
Dolgellau *Gwyn* 8 S16
Dolla *Tipperary* 39 S7
Dollar *Clack* 24 K16
Dolphinton *S Lanarks* 20 L17
Dolton *Devon* 3 W15
Dolwyddelan *Conwy* 8 R16
Donabate *Dublin* 37 R11
Donadea *Kildare* 37 R10
Donagh *Fermanagh* 32 P9
Donaghadee *Down* 33 N12
Donaghmore *Laois* 39 S8
Donaghmore *Tyrone* 33 N10
Donard *Wicklow* 40 R10
Doncaster *S Yorks* 16 Q21
Donegal *Donegal* 32 N7
Doneraile *Cork* 39 T6
Donhead St.Andrew
  Wilts 5 V19
Donington *Lincs* 12 S23
Donnington *Telford* 10 S19
Donohill *Tipperary* 39 S7
Donore *Meath* 37 Q11
Donoughmore *Cork* 39 U6
Dooagh *Mayo* 34 Q3
Doocharry *Donegal* 32 N7
Doogary *Cavan* 36 P8
Doogort *Mayo* 34 P3
Dooish *Tyrone* 32 N9
Doolin *Clare* 34 R5
Doon *Limerick* 39 S7
Doonaha *Clare* 38 S4
Doonbeg *Clare* 38 S4
Dorchester *Dorset* 5 W19
Dorchester *Oxon* 5 U21
Dores *H'land* 28 H15
Dorking *Surrey* 6 V23
Dornie *H'land* 27 H12
Dornoch *H'land* 28 G15
Dorridge *W Midlands* 11 T20
Dorstone *Heref'd* 10 T18
Douglas *Cork* 39 U7
Douglas *I/Man* 14 P15
Douglas *S Lanarks* 19 L16
Doune *Stirl* 24 K15
Dounreay *H'land* 28 E16
Dove Holes *Derby* 15 R20
Dover *Kent* 7 V26
Doveridge *Derby* 11 S20
Downham Market
  Norfolk 12 S24
Downham *Cambs* 12 T24
Downhill
  Londonderry 33 M10
Downies *Donegal* 32 M8
Downpatrick *Down* 33 P12
Downton *Wilts* 5 W20
Dowra *Leitrim* 32 P7
Drangan *Tipperary* 39 S8
Draperstown
  Londonderry 33 N10
Drayton *Norfolk* 13 S26
Dreenagh *Kerry* 38 T4
Dreghorn *N Ayrs* 19 L14

Drem *E Loth* 25 K18
Driffield *ER Yorks* 17 P23
Drigg *Cumb* 14 P17
Drimnin *H'land* 23 J12
Drimoleague *Cork* 38 U5
Drinagh *Cork* 38 U5
Dripsey *Cork* 39 U6
Drogheda *Louth* 37 Q11
Droitwich *Worcs* 10 T19
Dromahair *Leitrim* 32 P7
Dromara *Down* 33 P11
Dromard *Sligo* 32 P6
Dromcolliher *Limerick* 39 T6
Dromin *Louth* 37 Q11
Dromina *Cork* 39 T6
Dromineer *Tipperary* 35 S7
Dromiskin *Louth* 37 Q11
Dromkeen *Limerick* 39 S7
Dromod *Leitrim* 36 Q8
Dromore *Down* 33 P11
Dromore *Tyrone* 32 N9
Dromore West *Sligo* 35 P6
Dronfield *Derby* 16 R21
Drongan *E Ayrs* 19 M15
Druid *Denbs* 8 S17
Drum *Monaghan* 36 P9
Drumaduff
  Londonderry 33 N10
Drumahoe
  Londonderry 32 N9
Drumakilly *Tyrone* 32 N9
Drumbad *Longford* 36 Q8
Drumbadmeen
  Fermanagh 32 P8
Drumbear *Monaghan* 33 P10
Drumbeg *Donegal* 32 N8
Drumbeg *Down* 33 N12
Drumbeg *H'land* 27 F13
Drumbilla *Louth* 37 P11
Drumbo *Monaghan* 37 Q10
Drumcard
  Fermanagh 32 P8
Drumcliff *Sligo* 32 P6
Drumcondra *Dublin* 37 R11
Drumcondra *Meath* 37 Q10
Drumcoo *Monaghan* 32 P9
Drumcree
  Westmeath 36 Q9
Drumdallagh *Antrim* 33 M11
Drumfin *Sligo* 35 P7
Drumfree *Donegal* 32 M9
Drumgask *H'land* 24 H15
Drumjohn *Dumf/Gal* 19 M15
Drumkeeran *Leitrim* 36 P7
Drumlegagh *Tyrone* 32 N9
Drumlish *Longford* 36 Q8
Drummore *Dumf/Gal* 18 N14
Drumnacross
  Donegal 32 N8
Drumnadrochit
  H'land 28 H15
Drumquin *Tyrone* 32 N9
Drumramer
  Londonderry 33 M10
Drumsallan *Armagh* 33 P10
Drumsaragh
  Londonderry 33 N10
Drumshanbo *Leitrim* 36 P7
Drumskinny
  Fermanagh 32 N8
Drumsna *Leitrim* 36 Q7
Drumsurn
  Londonderry 33 M10
Drymen *Stirl* 24 K15
Drynoch *H'land* 26 H11
Dublin *Dublin* 37 R11
Duchally *H'land* 27 F14
Duddington
  Northants 12 S22
Dudley *W Midlands* 10 S19
Duffield *Derby* 11 S21
Dufftown *Moray* 29 H17
Dukinfield *Gtr Man* 15 R19
Duleek *Meath* 37 Q11
Dullingham *Cambs* 12 T24
Dulnain Bridge
  H'land 28 H16
Duloe *Cornw'l* 3 X15
Dulverton *Som'set* 4 V16
Dumbarton *W Dunb* 19 L14
Dumfries *Dumf/Gal* 20 M17
Dun Laoghaire *Dublin* 37 R11
Dunaff *Donegal* 32 M9
Dunans *Arg/Bute* 23 K13
Dunbar *E Loth* 25 K18
Dunbeath *H'land* 28 F17
Dunblane *Stirl* 24 K16
Dunboyne *Meath* 37 R11
Duncansby *H'land* 29 E17

Dunchurch *Warwick* 11 T21
Duncormick *Wexford* 40 T10
Dundalk *Louth* 37 P11
Dundee *Dundee C* 25 K18
Dunderrow *Cork* 39 U6
Dunderry *Meath* 37 Q10
Dundonald *Down* 33 N12
Dundonald *S Ayrs* 19 L14
Dundrennan
  Dumf/Gal 19 N16
Dundrod *Antrim* 33 N11
Dundrum *Dublin* 37 R11
Dundrum *Tipperary* 39 S7
Dundrum *Down* 33 P12
Dunecht *Aberds* 25 H19
Dunfanaghy *Donegal* 32 M8
Dunfermline *Fife* 24 K17
Dungannon *Tyrone* 33 N10
Dungarvan *Waterford* 39 T8
Dungiven
  Londonderry 33 N10
Dunglow *Donegal* 32 N7
Dungourney *Cork* 39 U7
Dunheeda *Meath* 37 Q10
Dunino *Fife* 25 K18
Dunipace *Falk* 24 K16
Dunkeld *Perth/Kinr* 24 J16
Dunkerrin *Offaly* 39 S8
Dunkineely *Donegal* 32 N7
Dunlavin *Wicklow* 40 R10
Dunleer *Louth* 37 Q11
Dunlop *E Ayrs* 19 L14
Dunloy *Antrim* 33 M11
Dunmanway *Cork* 38 U5
Dunmore East
  Waterford 40 T10
Dunmore *Galway* 35 Q6
Dunmurry *Antrim* 33 N11
Dunnamanagh
  Tyrone 32 N9
Dunnet *H'land* 28 E17
Dunning *Perth/Kinr* 24 K16
Dunnington *C/York* 17 Q22
Dunoon *Arg/Bute* 18 L14
Dunragit *Dumf/Gal* 18 N14
Duns *Scot Borders* 21 L19
Dunsany *Meath* 37 Q10
Dunsby *Lincs* 12 S23
Dunscore *Dumf/Gal* 19 M16
Dunsford *Devon* 4 W16
Dunshaughlin *Meath* 37 Q10
Dunstable *Beds* 6 U22
Dunster *Som'set* 4 V17
Dunston *Staffs* 10 S19
Dunsyre *S Lanarks* 20 L17
Dunure *S Ayrs* 19 M14
Dunvegan *H'land* 26 H10
Durham *Durham* 21 N20
Durness *H'land* 27 E14
Durrington *Wilts* 5 V20
Durrow Abbey *Offaly* 36 R8
Durrow *Laois* 40 S9
Durrus *Cork* 38 U4
Dursley *Glos* 5 U19
Dyan *Tyrone* 33 P10
Dyce *Aberd C* 25 H19
Dykehead *Angus* 25 J17
Dymchurch *Kent* 7 V26
Dymock *Glos* 10 U19
Dysart *Westmeath* 36 R9
Dysart *Fife* 25 K17
Dyserth *Denbs* 8 R17

E

Eaglescliffe *Stockton* 16 N21
Eaglesfield *Dumf/Gal* 20 M17
Eaglesham *E Renf* 19 L15
Eakring *Notts* 11 R22
Ealing *Gtr Lon* 6 U23
Earby *Lancs* 15 Q19
Eardisley *Heref'd* 10 T17
Eargantea
  Londonderry 33 M10
Earith *Cambs* 12 T24
Earl Shilton *Leics* 11 S21
Earl Soham *Suffolk* 13 T26
Earls Barton
  Northants 12 T22
Earl's Colne *Essex* 13 U25
Earlsferry *Fife* 25 K18
Earlston
  Scot Borders 21 L18
Earlstown *Galway* 35 R7
Earsdon *Tyne/Wear* 21 M21

Easebourne
  W Sussex 6 W22
Easington Colliery
  Durham 21 N21
Easington *Durham* 21 N21
Easington *ER Yorks* 17 Q24
Easingwold *N Yorks* 16 P21
Easky *Sligo* 35 P6
East Bergholt *Suffolk* 13 U26
East Brent *Som'set* 4 V18
East Bridgford *Notts* 11 S22
East Calder *W Loth* 20 L17
East Cowes *I/Wight* 5 W21
East Cowton *N Yorks* 16 P20
East Dean *E Sussex* 6 W24
East Dereham
  Norfolk 13 S25
East Grinstead
  W Sussex 6 V24
East Harling *Norfolk* 13 T25
East Horsley *Surrey* 6 V23
East Ilsley *W Berks* 5 U21
East Kilbride
  S Lanarks 19 L15
East Leake *Notts* 11 S21
East Linton *E Loth* 25 L18
East Looe *Cornw'l* 3 X15
East Markham *Notts* 17 R22
East Norton *Leics* 11 S22
East Oakley *Hants* 5 V21
East Wemyss *Fife* 25 K17
East Wittering
  W Sussex 6 W22
East Witton *N Yorks* 15 P20
East Woodhay *Hants* 5 V21
Eastbourne *E Sussex* 7 W24
Eastchurch *Kent* 7 V25
Eastfield *N Yorks* 17 P23
Eastleigh *Hants* 5 W21
Eastnor *Heref'd* 10 T19
Easton *Dorset* 5 W19
Easton *Northants* 12 S22
Easton-in-Gordano
  N Som'set 4 V18
Eastry *Kent* 7 V26
Eastwood *Notts* 11 R21
Eaton Socon *Cambs* 12 T23
Eaton *Leics* 11 S22
Ebberston *N Yorks* 17 P22
Ebbw Vale *Bl Gwent* 4 U17
Ecclaw *Scot Borders* 25 L19
Ecclefechan
  Dumf/Gal 20 M17
Eccleshall *Staffs* 10 S19
Echt *Aberds* 25 H19
Eckington *Derby* 16 R21
Eckington *Worcs* 10 T19
Edderton *H'land* 28 G15
Eden *Antrim* 33 N12
Edenaveagh
  Fermanagh 32 N8
Edenbridge *Kent* 6 V24
Edenderry *Offaly* 36 R9
Ederny *Fermanagh* 32 N8
Edgeworthstown
  Longford 36 Q8
Edmond *Telford* 10 S19
Edinburgh *C/Edinb* 25 L17
Edington *Wilts* 5 V19
Edmondstown *Louth* 37 Q10
Edmundbyers
  Durham 21 N20
Edwinstowe *Notts* 11 R21
Edzell *Angus* 25 J18
Egham *Surrey* 6 V22
Eglinton *Londonderry* 32 M9
Eglish *Tyrone* 33 P10
Eglwyswrw *Pembs* 9 T14
Egremont *Cumb* 14 P16
Egton *N Yorks* 17 P22
Eighter *Cavan* 36 Q9
Eilean Iarmain *H'land* 23 H12
Elan Village *Powys* 9 T16
Elgin *Moray* 28 G17
Elgol *H'land* 22 H11
Elham *Kent* 7 V26
Elie *Fife* 25 K18
Elishaw *Northum* 21 M19
Elland *W Yorks* 15 Q20
Ellesmere Port *Ches* 15 R18
Ellesmere *Shrops* 10 S18
Ellington *Northum* 21 M20
Ellistrin *Donegal* 32 N8
Ellon *Aberds* 29 H19
Elmswell *Suffolk* 13 T25
Elphin *Roscommon* 35 Q7
Elphin *H'land* 27 F13
Elsdon *Northum* 21 M19

Elsenham *Essex* 12 U24
Elstead *Surrey* 6 V22
Elston *Notts* 11 S22
Elvanfoot *S Lanarks* 20 M16
Elveden *Suffolk* 13 T25
Elvington *C/York* 17 Q22
Elworth *Ches* 10 R19
Ely *Cambs* 12 T24
Embleton *Northum* 21 M20
Embo *H'land* 28 G15
Emly *Tipperary* 39 T7
Emmoo *Roscommon* 36 Q7
Empingham *Rutl'd* 12 S22
Emsworth *Hants* 6 W22
Emyvale *Monaghan* 33 P10
Enderby *Leics* 11 S21
Endon *Staffs* 10 R19
Enfield *Gtr Lon* 6 U23
Ennis *Clare* 39 S6
Enniscorthy *Wexford* 40 S10
Enniskean *Cork* 39 U6
Enniskerry *Wicklow* 37 R11
Enniskillen
  Fermanagh 32 P8
Ennistimon *Clare* 34 S5
Enstone *Oxon* 11 U21
Enterkinfoot
  Dumf/Gal 19 M16
Epping *Essex* 6 U24
Epsom *Surrey* 6 V23
Epworth *N Lincs* 17 Q22
Eriboll *H'land* 28 F14
Errill *Laois* 39 S8
Errogie *H'land* 28 H15
Errol *Perth/Kinr* 25 K17
Erskine *Renf* 19 L15
Escrick *N Yorks* 16 Q21
Esh Winning *Durham* 21 N20
Esher *Surrey* 6 V23
Eskdalemuir
  Dumf/Gal 20 M17
Essexford *Monaghan* 37 Q10
Eston
  Redcar/Clevel'd 21 N21
Etchingham
  E Sussex 7 V24
Eton *Windsor* 6 V22
Ettington *Warwick* 11 T21
Etwall *Derby* 11 S20
Euxton *Lancs* 15 Q18
Evanton *H'land* 28 G15
Evercreech *Som'set* 5 V19
Everleigh *Wilts* 5 V20
Evershot *Dorset* 4 W18
Evesham *Worcs* 11 T20
Ewell *Surrey* 6 V23
Ewhurst *Surrey* 6 V23
Ewyas Harold
  Heref'd 10 U18
Exbourne *Devon* 4 W16
Exeter *Devon* 4 W16
Exford *Som'set* 4 V16
Exminster *Devon* 4 W17
Exmouth *Devon* 4 W17
Exton *Rutl'd* 12 S22
Eyam *Derby* 16 R20
Eye Peterbro* 12 S23
Eye *Suffolk* 13 T26
Eyemouth
  Scot Borders 21 L19
Eynsford *Kent* 6 V24
Eynsham *Oxon* 5 U21
Eyrecourt *Galway* 36 R7

F

Faddiley *Ches* 10 R18
Fairbourne *Gwyn* 8 S15
Fairford *Glos* 5 U20
Fairlie *N Ayrs* 18 L14
Fairlight *E Sussex* 7 W25
Fakenham *Norfolk* 13 S25
Fala *Midloth* 20 L18
Falcarragh *Donegal* 32 M7
Faldingworth *Lincs* 17 R23
Falkirk *Falk* 24 K16
Falkland *Fife* 25 K17
Fallmore *Mayo* 34 P3
Falmer *E Sussex* 6 W23
Falmouth *Cornw'l* 2 X13
Falstone *Northum* 21 M19
Fardrum *Westmeath* 36 R8
Fareham *Hants* 5 W21
Faringdon *Oxon* 5 U20
Farnborough *Hants* 6 V22

Farnborough		
W Berks	5	U21
Farndon Ches	10	R18
Farnham Surrey	6	V22
Farnworth Gtr Man	15	Q19
Farr H'land	28	H15
Farranfore Kerry	38	T4
Fasag H'land	27	G12
Faslane Arg/Bute	23	K14
Fauldhouse W Loth	20	L16
Faversham Kent	7	V25
Fawley Hants	5	W21
Fazeley Staffs	11	S20
Feakle Clare	35	S6
Fearn H'land	28	G16
Fearnan Perth/Kinr	24	J15
Feckenham Worcs	11	T20
Fedamore Limerick	39	S6
Feeard Clare	38	S4
Feenhanagh Limerick	39	T6
Feeny Londonderry	33	N9
Felixstowe Suffolk	13	S26
Felton Northum	21	M20
Feltwell Norfolk	13	T25
Fenagh Leitrim	36	P8
Fenit Kerry	38	T4
Fennagh Carlow	40	S10
Fenny Bentley Derby	11	R20
Fenny Compton		
Warwick	11	T21
Fenny Stratford		
M/Keynes	12	U22
Fenwick E Ayrs	19	L15
Feock Cornw'l	2	X13
Feolin Ferry Arg/Bute	18	L11
Ferbane Offaly	36	R8
Fermoy Cork	39	T7
Ferndown Dorset	5	W20
Fernhurst W Sussex	6	V22
Fernilea H'land	26	H11
Ferns Wexford	40	S11
Ferryhill Durham	21	N20
Ferryside Carms	9	U15
Fethard Tipperary	39	T8
Fethard Wexford	40	T10
Fettercairn Aberds	25	J18
Ffestiniog Gwyn	8	S16
Fiddown Kilkenny	40	T9
Filby Norfolk	13	S27
Filey N Yorks	17	P23
Fillongley Warwick	11	T20
Filton S Glos	4	U18
Fincarn Londonderry	33	N10
Fincham Norfolk	12	S24
Finchingfield Essex	12	U24
Finchley Gtr Lon	6	U23
Findhorn Moray	28	G16
Findochty Moray	29	G18
Findon W Sussex	6	W23
Finedon Northants	12	T22
Finglas Dublin	37	R11
Finnea Westmeath	36	Q9
Finningley S Yorks	17	R22
Finnis Down	33	P11
Fintona Tyrone	32	P9
Fintown Donegal	32	N7
Fintry Stirl	24	K15
Finvoy Antrim	33	M11
Fionnphort Arg/Bute	22	K11
Fishbourne I/Wight	5	W21
Fishguard Pembs	9	U14
Fishnish Arg/Bute	23	J12
Fishtoft Lincs	12	S24
Five Alley Offaly	36	R8
Fivemiletown Tyrone	32	P9
Flagmount Clare	35	S6
Flamborough		
ER Yorks	17	P23
Fleet Hants	6	V22
Fleetwood Lancs	15	Q17
Flimby Cumb	20	N17
Flint Flints	15	R17
Flitwick Beds	12	U22
Flodden Northum	21	L19
Flookburgh Cumb	15	P18
Fochabers Moray	29	G17
Foel Powys	8	S17
Folkestone Kent	7	V26
Fontmell Magna		
Dorset	5	W19
Fontstown Kildare	40	R10
Ford Wexford	40	S11
Ford Arg/Bute	23	K13
Forden Powys	10	S17
Fordham Cambs	12	T24
Fordingbridge Hants	5	W20
Fordstown Meath	37	Q10
Fordyce Aberds	29	G18
Fore Westmeath	36	Q9
Forest Row E Sussex	6	V24
Forfar Angus	25	J18
Forgney Longford	36	Q8
Forkill Armagh	37	P11
Formby Mersey	15	Q17
Forres Moray	28	G16
Forsinain H'land	28	F16
Forsinard H'land	28	F16
Fort Augustus H'land	24	H14
Fort William H'land	23	J13
Forth S Lanarks	20	L16
Fortrie Aberds	29	G18
Fortrose H'land	28	G15
Fortuneswell Dorset	5	W19
Fothergill Cumb	20	N17
Fotheringhay		
Northants	12	S23
Foulden		
Scot Borders	21	L19
Foulkesmill Wexford	40	T10
Foulsham Norfolk	13	S26
Fountain Cross Clare	38	S5
Fountainhall		
Scot Borders	20	L18
Four Mile House		
Roscommon	35	Q7
Fovant Wilts	5	V20
Fowey Cornw'l	2	X14
Fownhope Heref'd	10	T18
Foxdale I/Man	14	P14
Foxford Mayo	35	Q5
Foyers H'land	24	H15
Foygh Longford	36	Q8
Foynes Limerick	38	S5
Fraddon Cornw'l	2	X14
Framlingham Suffolk	13	T26
Frampton on Severn		
Glos	5	U19
Frankville Down	33	P12
Frant E Sussex	7	V24
Fraserburgh Aberds	29	G19
Freckleton Lancs	15	Q18
Freemount Cork	39	T6
Freethorpe Norfolk	13	S27
Fremington Devon	3	V15
Frenchpark		
Roscommon	35	Q7
Frensham Surrey	6	V22
Freshford Kilkenny	40	S9
Freshwater I/Wight	5	W20
Fressingfield Suffolk	13	T26
Freswick H'land	29	E17
Freuchie Fife	25	K17
Friday Bridge Cambs	12	S24
Fridaythorpe		
ER Yorks	17	P22
Frimley Surrey	6	V22
Frinton-on-Sea Essex	7	U26
Friockheim Angus	25	J18
Frizington Cumb	20	N17
Frodsham Ches	15	R18
Frome Som'set	5	V19
Frongoch Gwyn	8	S16
Froxfield Wilts	5	V20
Fuerty Roscommon	35	Q7
Fulbourn Cambs	12	T24
Fulford C/York	16	Q21
Fulwood Lancs	15	Q18
Furnace Arg/Bute	23	K13
Fybagh Kerry	38	T4
Fyfield Essex	7	U24
Fyvie Aberds	29	H19

G

Gaerwen Angl	8	R15
Gaick Lodge H'land	24	J15
Gailey Staffs	10	S19
Gainford Durham	21	N20
Gainsborough Lincs	17	R22
Gairloch H'land	27	G12
Gairlochy H'land	23	J14
Galashiels		
Scot Borders	20	L18
Galbally Limerick	39	T7
Galgate Lancs	15	Q18
Galmisdale H'land	22	J11
Galmoy Kilkenny	39	S8
Galmpton Torbay	3	X16
Galston E Ayrs	19	L15
Galway Galway	35	R5
Gamlingay Cambs	12	T23
Garbally Galway	35	R7
Garbhallt Arg/Bute	23	K13
Garboldisham		
Norfolk	13	T25
Gardenstown Aberds	29	G19
Garelochhead		
Arg/Bute	23	K14
Garforth W Yorks	16	Q21
Gargrave N Yorks	15	Q19
Gargunnock Stirl	24	K15
Garlieston Dumf/Gal	19	N15
Garmouth Moray	29	G17
Garrane Cork	38	U5
Garrison Fermanagh	32	P7
Garristown Dublin	37	Q11
Garrow Perth/Kinr	24	J16
Garryvoe Cork	39	U7
Garsdale Head		
Cumb	15	P19
Garstang Lancs	15	Q18
Garston Mersey	15	R18
Garton-on-the-Wolds		
ER Yorks	17	P22
Garvagh		
Londonderry	33	N10
Garvaghy Down	33	P11
Garvaghy Tyrone	32	P9
Garvald E Loth	25	L18
Garvary Fermanagh	32	P8
Garve H'land	28	G14
Gatehouse of Fleet		
Dumf/Gal	19	N15
Gateshead		
Tyne/Wear	21	N20
Gatley Gtr Man	15	R19
Gattabaun Kilkenny	40	S9
Gawthwaite Cumb	15	P17
Gay Brook		
Westmeath	36	R9
Gaydon Warwick	11	T21
Gayton Norfolk	13	S25
Gaywood Norfolk	12	S24
Gearraidh na h-		
Aibhne W Isles	26	F10
Geary H'land	26	G10
Geashill Offaly	36	R9
Geddington		
Northants	12	T22
Gedney Lincs	12	S24
Georgeham Devon	3	V15
Gerrards Cross		
Bucks	6	U22
Gifford E Loth	25	L18
Giggleswick N Yorks	15	P19
Gilford Down	33	P11
Gillingham Dorset	5	V19
Gillingham Medway	7	V25
Gilmerton Perth/Kinr	24	K16
Gilsland Northum	21	N18
Gilwern Monmouths	4	U17
Giosla W Isles	26	F10
Girton Cambs	12	T24
Girvan S Ayrs	18	M14
Gisburn Lancs	15	Q19
Gladestry Powys	10	T17
Glamis Angus	25	J17
Glanaman Carms	9	U16
Glandore Cork	38	U5
Glanton Northum	21	M20
Glanworth Cork	39	T7
Glasbury Powys	10	T17
Glasdrumman Down	37	P12
Glasgow C/Glasg	19	L15
Glaslough Monaghan	33	P10
Glasnevin Dublin	37	R11
Glassan Westmeath	36	R8
Glasserton Dumf/Gal	19	N15
Glasson Lancs	15	Q19
Glastonbury Som'set	4	V18
Glastry Down	33	P13
Glemsford Suffolk	13	T25
Glen Donegal	32	M8
Glen Fermanagh	32	P7
Glenade Leitrim	32	P7
Glenamoy Mayo	34	P4
Glenariff Antrim	33	M11
Glenarm Antrim	33	N12
Glenavy Antrim	33	N11
Glenbarr Arg/Bute	18	L12
Glenbeigh Kerry	38	T4
Glenborrodale H'land	23	J12
Glenbrittle H'land	22	H11
Glencaple Dumf/Gal	20	N16
Glencar Kerry	38	T4
Glencarse Perth/Kinr	24	K17
Glencoe H'land	23	J13
Glencolumbkille		
Donegal	32	N6
Glendalough Wicklow	40	R11
Glendoll Lodge		
Angus	25	J17
Glendree Clare	39	S6
Gleneagles		
Perth/Kinr	24	K16
Glenealy Wicklow	40	S11
Gleneely Donegal	32	M9
Glenelg H'land	23	H12
Glenfarn Longford	32	P8
Glenfesk Kerry	38	T5
Glenfinnan H'land	23	J13
Glengarriff Cork	38	U4
Glengavlen Cavan	32	P8
Glengormly Antrim	33	N12
Glenluce Dumf/Gal	18	N14
Glenmaye I/Man	14	P14
Glenmore Lodge		
H'land	24	H16
Glennamaddy		
Galway	35	Q6
Glenoe Antrim	33	N12
Glenprosen Lodge		
Angus	25	J17
Glenrothes Fife	25	K17
Glenstal Abbey		
Limerick	39	S7
Glenstriven Arg/Bute	18	L13
Glentane Galway	35	R6
Glenties Donegal	32	N7
Glentrool Village		
Dumf/Gal	19	M14
Glenville Cork	39	T7
Glenwhilly Dumf/Gal	18	M14
Glin Limerick	38	S5
Glinsk Galway	34	R4
Glinsk Galway	35	Q7
Glinton Peterboro	12	S23
Glossop Derby	15	R20
Gloucester Glos	10	U19
Glusburn N Yorks	15	Q20
Glyn Ceiriog Wrex	10	S17
Glyn Neath		
Neath P Talb	9	U16
Glyncorrwg		
Neath P Talb	9	U16
Glynde E Sussex	6	W24
Glyndyfrdwy Denbs	10	S17
Glynn Carlow	40	S10
Glynn Antrim	33	N12
Gnosall Staffs	10	S19
Goathland N Yorks	17	P22
Gobowen Shrops	10	S17
Godalming Surrey	6	V22
Godmanchester		
Cambs	12	T23
Godshill I/Wight	5	W21
Godstone Surrey	6	V23
Golden Tipperary	39	T8
Goldhanger Essex	7	U25
Goleen Cork	39	V4
Golspie H'land	28	G16
Goodrich Heref'd	10	U18
Goodwick Pembs	9	T13
Goodwood		
W Sussex	6	W22
Goole ER Yorks	17	Q22
Goonhavern Cornw'l	2	X13
Gordon Scot Borders	21	L18
Gorebridge Midloth	20	L17
Goresbridge Kilkenny	40	S10
Gorey Wexford	40	S11
Gorey Chan Is	2	Z19
Goring Oxon	5	U21
Goring-by-Sea		
W Sussex	6	W23
Gorleston Norfolk	13	S27
Gormanstown Meath	37	Q11
Gorran Haven		
Cornw'l	2	X14
Gorseinon Swan	9	U15
Gorslas Carms	9	U15
Gort Galway	35	S6
Gortahork Donegal	32	M7
Gorteen Galway	35	Q6
Gorteen Galway	35	R6
Gorteen Sligo	35	Q6
Gorteen Waterford	39	T8
Gorteng Galway	35	R7
Gortin Tyrone	32	N9
Gortnacross		
Londonderry	33	N10
Gortroe Cork	39	T6
Gortymadden		
Galway	35	R7
Gosberton Lincs	12	S23
Gosfield Essex	13	U25
Gosforth Cumb	15	P17
Gosport Hants	5	W21
Goswick Northum	21	L20
Gotham Notts	11	S21
Goudhurst Kent	7	V24
Gourdon Aberds	25	J19
Gourock Invercl	18	L14
Gowerton Swan	9	U15
Gowlaun Galway	34	Q4
Gowran Kilkenny	40	S9
Grabhair W Isles	26	F11
Graghil Mayo	34	P4
Graigue Laois	40	S10
Graiguenamanagh		
Kilkenny	40	S10
Grain Medway	7	V25
Grainthorpe Lincs	17	R24
Grampound Cornw'l	2	X14
Gramsdal W Isles	26	H9
Granard Longford	36	Q9
Grange Kilkenny	40	S9
Grange Roscommon	36	Q7
Grange Sligo	32	P6
Grangebellew Louth	37	Q11
Grangemouth Falk	24	K16
Grange-over-Sands		
Cumb	15	P18
Grantham Lincs	12	S22
Grantown-on-Spey		
H'land	28	H16
Grantshouse		
Scot Borders	21	L19
Granville Tyrone	33	P10
Grasby Lincs	17	Q23
Grasmere Cumb	15	P18
Grassington N Yorks	15	P20
Grateley Hants	5	V20
Gravesend Kent	7	V24
Grayrigg Cumb	15	P18
Grays Thurr'k	7	V24
Grayshott Hants	6	V22
Great Ayton N Yorks	16	N21
Great Baddow Essex	7	U25
Great Badminton		
S Glos	5	U19
Great Barford Beds	12	T23
Great Bentley Essex	7	U26
Great Bridgeford		
Staffs	10	S19
Great Broughton		
N Yorks	16	P21
Great Chesterford		
Essex	12	T24
Great Clifton Cumb	20	N17
Great Dunmow		
Essex	7	U24
Great Eccleston		
Lancs	15	Q18
Great Ellingham		
Norfolk	13	S25
Great Gidding		
Cambs	12	T23
Great Harwood		
Lancs	15	Q19
Great Horwood		
Bucks	11	U22
Great Malvern Worcs	10	T19
Great Massingham		
Norfolk	13	S25
Great Missenden		
Bucks	6	U22
Great Oakley Essex	7	U26
Great Sampford		
Essex	12	U24
Great Shefford		
W Berks	5	V21
Great Shelford		
Cambs	12	T24
Great Somerford		
Wilts	5	U19
Great Staunton		
Cambs	12	T23
Great Torrington		
Devon	3	W15
Great Wakering		
Essex	7	U25
Great Waltham Essex	7	U24
Great Witley Worcs	10	T19
Great Yarmouth		
Norfolk	13	S27
Greatham Hartlep'l	21	N21
Greatstone-on-Sea		
Kent	7	W25
Green Hammerton		
N Yorks	16	P21
Greencastle Donegal	33	M10
Greencastle Down	37	P11
Greencastle Tyrone	33	N9
Greenhead Northum	21	N18
Greenholm E Ayrs	19	L15
Greenisland Antrim	33	N12
Greenlaw		
Scot Borders	21	L19

Greenloaning
  Perth/Kinr 24 K16
Greenock Invercl 18 L14
Greenodd Cumb 15 P17
Greenore Louth 37 P11
Greenway Pembs 9 U14
Greenwich Gtr Lon 6 V24
Greevagh Sligo 35 P7
Gretna Green
  Dumf/Gal 20 M17
Gretna Dumf/Gal 20 N17
Gretton Northants 12 S22
Greyabbey Down 33 N12
Greysteel
  Londonderry 33 M9
Greystoke Cumb 20 N18
Greystones Wicklow 37 R11
Grimsby NE Lincs 17 Q23
Grizebeck Cumb 15 P17
Groby Leics 11 S21
Groomsport Down 33 N12
Grove Oxon 5 U21
Grundisburgh Suffolk 13 T26
Guard Bridge Fife 25 K18
Gubaveeny Cavan 32 P8
Gudderstown Louth 37 Q10
Guestling Green
  E Sussex 7 W25
Guildford Surrey 6 V22
Guildtown Perth/Kinr 24 K17
Guilsfield Powys 10 S17
Guisborough
  Redcar/Clevel'd 16 N21
Guiseley W Yorks 16 Q20
Gulladuff
  Londonderry 33 N10
Gullane E Loth 25 K18
Gunnerside N Yorks 15 P19
Gunnislake Cornw'l 3 W15
Gwalchmai Angl 8 R15
Gwaun-Cae-Gurwen
  Neath P Talb 9 U16
Gwbert-on-Sea
  Ceredig'n 9 T14
Gweedore Donegal 32 M7
Gweek Cornw'l 2 X13
Gwennap Cornw'l 2 X13
Gwessalia Mayo 34 P4
Gwyddelwern Denbs 8 R17
Gwytherin Conwy 8 R16

H

Hacketstown Carlow 40 S10
Hackney Gtr Lon 6 U23
Hackthorpe Cumb 21 N18
Haddenham Bucks 6 U22
Haddenham Cambs 12 T24
Haddington E Loth 25 L18
Haddiscoe Norfolk 13 S27
Hadleigh Essex 7 U25
Hadleigh Suffolk 13 T25
Hadlow Kent 7 V24
Hadnall Shrops 10 S18
Hagworthingham
  Lincs 17 R24
Hailsham E Sussex 7 W24
Hainton Lincs 17 R23
Halberton Devon 4 W17
Halesowen
  W Midlands 10 T19
Halesworth Suffolk 13 T27
Halford Warwick 11 T20
Halifax W Yorks 15 Q20
Halkirk H'land 28 E16
Halland E Sussex 6 W24
Hallow Worcs 10 T19
Hallworthy Cornw'l 2 W14
Halstead Essex 13 U25
Halton Lancs 15 P18
Haltwhistle Northum 21 N19
Halwill Junction
  Devon 3 W15
Hambledon Hants 5 W21
Hamble-le-Rice
  Hants 5 W21
Hambleton Lancs 15 Q18
Hambleton N Yorks 16 Q21
Hamerton Cambs 12 T23
Hamiltownbawn
  Armagh 33 P10
Hamilton S Lanarks 19 L15
Hammersmith &
  Fulham Gtr Lon 6 V23
Hampstead Norreys
  W Berks 5 V21

Hampton in Arden
  W Midlands 11 T20
Hamstreet Kent 7 V25
Handcross W Sussex 6 V23
Hannington Hants 5 V21
Harbury Warwick 11 T21
Harby Leics 11 S22
Hardingstone
  Northants 12 T22
Harewood W Yorks 16 Q20
Haringey Gtr Lon 6 V23
Harlech Gwyn 8 S15
Harleston Norfolk 13 T26
Harlow Essex 6 U24
Harpenden Herts 6 U23
Harrietfield Perth/Kinr 24 K16
Harrietsham Kent 7 V25
Harrington Cumb 20 N16
Harris H'land 22 J11
Harrogate N Yorks 16 P20
Harrold Beds 12 T22
Harrow Gtr Lon 6 U23
Harston Cambs 12 T24
Hartest Suffolk 13 T25
Harthill E Sussex 6 V24
Harthill N Lanarks 19 L16
Hartington Derby 11 R20
Hartland Devon 3 W15
Hartlebury Worcs 10 T19
Hartlepool Hartlep'l 21 N21
Hartley Kent 7 V24
Hartley Northum 21 M21
Hartley Wintney
  Hants 6 V22
Hartpury Glos 10 U19
Hartshill Warwick 11 S20
Harvington Worcs 11 T20
Harwell Oxon 5 U21
Harwich Essex 13 U26
Harworth Notts 16 R21
Haselbury Plucknett
  Som'set 4 W18
Haslemere Surrey 6 V22
Haslingden Lancs 15 Q19
Hassocks W Sussex 6 W23
Hastigrow H'land 29 E17
Hastings E Sussex 7 W25
Haswell Durham 21 N21
Hatch Beauchamp
  Som'set 4 W18
Hatfield Heath Essex 6 U24
Hatfield Peverel
  Essex 6 U25
Hatfield Herts 6 U23
Hatfield S Yorks 17 Q22
Hatherleigh Devon 3 W15
Hathersage Derby 16 R20
Hatton Aberds 29 H20
Hatton Derby 11 S20
Haugh of Urr
  Dumf/Gal 19 N16
Haughley Suffolk 13 T25
Haughton Staffs 10 S19
Havant Hants 6 W22
Haverfordwest
  Pembs 9 U14
Haverhill Suffolk 12 T24
Haverigg Cumb 14 P17
Havering Gtr Lon 6 U24
Hawarden Flints 10 R17
Hawes N Yorks 15 P19
Hawick Scot Borders 20 M18
Hawkchurch Devon 4 W18
Hawkesbury Upton
  S Glos 5 U19
Hawkhurst Kent 7 V25
Hawkinge Kent 7 V26
Hawkshead Cumb 15 P18
Hawnby N Yorks 16 P21
Haworth W Yorks 15 Q20
Hawsker N Yorks 16 P21
Haxby C/York 16 P21
Haxey N Lincs 17 R22
Haydon Bridge
  Northum 21 N19
Hayfield Derby 15 R20
Hayle Cornw'l 2 X13
Hay-on-Wye Powys 10 T17
Hayton Cumb 20 N18
Hayton ER Yorks 17 Q22
Haywards Heath
  W Sussex 6 W23
Hazel Grove Gtr Man 15 R19
Hazlemere Bucks 6 U22
Heacham Norfolk 12 S24
Headcorn Kent 7 V25
Headford Galway 35 R5
Headley Hants 6 V22

Heanor Derby 11 R21
Heath End Hants 5 V21
Heathfield E Sussex 7 W24
Hebburn Tyne/Wear 21 N20
Hebden Bridge
  W Yorks 15 Q19
Heckington Lincs 12 S23
Hedge End Hants 5 W21
Hednesford Staffs 11 S20
Hedon ER Yorks 17 Q23
Heighington D'lington 21 N20
Heilam H'land 28 E14
Helensburgh
  Arg/Bute 24 K14
Hellifield N Yorks 15 P19
Helmsdale H'land 28 F16
Helmsley N Yorks 16 P21
Helperby N Yorks 16 P21
Helpringham Lincs 12 S23
Helsby Ches 15 R18
Helston Cornw'l 2 X13
Hemel Hempstead
  Herts 6 U23
Hemingbrough
  N Yorks 17 Q22
Hempnall Norfolk 13 S26
Hempton Norfolk 13 S25
Hemsby Norfolk 13 S27
Hemsworth W Yorks 16 Q21
Hemyock Devon 4 W17
Henfield W Sussex 6 W23
Hengoed Caerph 4 U17
Henley-in-Arden
  Warwick 11 T20
Henley-on-Thames
  Oxon 6 U22
Henllan Denbs 8 R17
Henlow Beds 12 T23
Henstridge Som'set 5 W19
Herbertstown
  Limerick 39 S7
Herbrandston Pembs 9 U13
Hereford Heref'd 10 T18
Heriot Scot Borders 20 L18
Hermitage W Berks 5 V21
Herne Bay Kent 7 V26
Herstmonceux
  E Sussex 7 W24
Hertford Herts 6 U23
Hessle Kingston/Hull 17 Q23
Heswall Mersey 15 R17
Hethersett Norfolk 13 S26
Hetton-le-Hole
  Tyne/Wear 21 N21
Hexham Northum 21 N19
Heybridge Essex 7 U25
Heysham Lancs 15 P18
Heytesbury Wilts 5 V19
Heywood Gtr Man 15 Q19
Hibaldstow N Lincs 17 Q22
High Bentham
  N Yorks 15 P19
High Bickington
  Devon 3 W15
High Ercall Telford 10 S18
High Hesket Cumb 20 N18
High Legh Ches 15 R19
High Wycombe
  Bucks 6 U22
Higham Ferrers
  Northants 12 T22
Higham Kent 7 V24
Highbridge Som'set 4 V18
Highclere Hants 5 V21
Highley Shrops 10 T19
Hightae Dumf/Gal 20 M17
Highworth Swindon 5 U20
Hilborough Norfolk 13 S25
Hildenborough Kent 6 V24
Hilgay Norfolk 12 S24
Hillingdon Gtr Lon 6 U23
Hillington Norfolk 13 S25
Hillsborough Down 33 P11
Hilltown Down 33 P11
Hilmarton Wilts 5 V20
Hilton Derby 11 S20
Hinckley Leics 11 S21
Hinderwell N Yorks 17 N22
Hindhead Surrey 6 V22
Hindley Gtr Man 15 Q18
Hindon Wilts 5 V19
Hingham Norfolk 13 S25
Hinstock Shrops 10 S19
Hirwaun Rh Cyn Taff 9 U17
Histon Cambs 12 T24
Hitchin Herts 12 U23
Hockley Essex 7 U25
Hockliffe Beds 12 U22
Hoddesdon Herts 6 U23

Hodnet Shrops 10 S18
Hoff Cumb 21 N18
Holbeach Lincs 12 S24
Holbrook Suffolk 13 U26
Holbury Hants 5 W21
Holford Som'set 4 V17
Holkham Norfolk 13 S25
Holland on Sea
  Essex 7 U26
Hollym ER Yorks 17 Q24
Hollymount Mayo 35 Q5
Hollywood Wicklow 37 R10
Holme-on-Spalding-
  moor ER Yorks 17 Q22
Holmer Heref'd 10 T18
Holmes Chapel Ches 10 R19
Holmfirth W Yorks 15 Q20
Holsworthy Devon 3 W15
Holt Norfolk 13 S26
Holt Wrex 10 R18
Holycross Limerick 39 S6
Holycross Tipperary 39 S8
Holyhead Angl 8 R14
Holywell Flints 15 R17
Holywood Down 33 N12
Honington Lincs 12 S22
Honiton Devon 4 W17
Hoo Medway 7 V25
Hook Norton Oxon 11 U21
Hook Hants 6 V22
Hope Flints 10 R17
Hope under Dinmore
  Heref'd 10 T18
Hopeman Moray 28 G17
Horam E Sussex 7 W24
Horden Durham 21 N21
Horley Surrey 6 V23
Horncastle Lincs 17 R23
Horndean Hants 6 W21
Horningsham Wilts 5 V19
Hornsea ER Yorks 17 Q23
Horrabridge Devon 3 X15
Horringer Suffolk 13 T25
Horseleap
  Crossroads
  Galway 35 R6
Horseleap Offaly 36 R8
Horsey Norfolk 13 S27
Horsford Norfolk 13 S26
Horsforth W Yorks 16 Q20
Horsham St. Faith
  Norfolk 13 S26
Horsham W Sussex 6 V23
Horsted Keynes
  W Sussex 6 V23
Horton in Ribblesdale
  N Yorks 15 P19
Horton Northants 11 T22
Horton Som'set 4 W18
Horwich Gtr Man 15 Q18
Hospital Limerick 39 T7
Houghton Regis
  Beds 12 U22
Houghton Cumb 20 N18
Houghton-le-Spring
  Tyne/Wear 21 N21
Hounslow Gtr Lon 6 V23
Hove Brighton/Hove 6 W23
Hoveton Norfolk 13 S26
Hovingham N Yorks 17 P22
Howden ER Yorks 17 Q22
Howpasley
  Scot Borders 20 M17
Howth Dublin 37 R11
Hoxne Suffolk 13 T26
Hoylake Mersey 15 R17
Hucknall Notts 11 R21
Huddersfield
  W Yorks 15 Q20
Hugh Town I/Scilly 2 Y11
Hulland Ward Derby 11 R20
Hullavington Wilts 5 U19
Hullbridge Essex 7 U25
Hulme End Staffs 11 R20
Humberston
  NE Lincs 17 Q23
Humshaugh Northum 21 M19
Hundred House
  Powys 10 T17
Hungerford W Berks 5 V20
Hunmanby N Yorks 17 P23
Hunstanton Norfolk 12 S24
Hunterston N Ayrs 18 L14
Huntford
  Scot Borders 20 M17
Huntingdon Cambs 12 T23
Huntley Glos 10 U19
Huntly Aberds 29 H18
Hurlers Cross Clare 39 S6

Hurlford E Ayrs 19 L15
Hurn Dorset 5 W20
Hursley Hants 5 V21
Hurstbourne Tarrant
  Hants 5 V21
Hurstpierpoint
  W Sussex 6 W23
Hurworth-on-Tees
  D'lington 16 P20
Husbands Bosworth
  Leics 11 T21
Husinish W Isles 26 G9
Huttoft Lincs 17 R24
Hutton Cranswick
  ER Yorks 17 Q23
Hutton Rudby
  N Yorks 16 P21
Hutton-le-Hole
  N Yorks 17 P22
Huyton Mersey 15 R18
Hyde Gtr Man 15 R19
Hynish Arg/Bute 22 K10
Hythe Hants 5 W21
Hythe Kent 7 V26

I

Ibsey Hants 5 W20
Ibstock Leics 11 S21
Icklingham Suffolk 13 T25
Idmiston Wilts 5 V20
Ilchester Som'set 4 W18
Ilderton Northum 21 M20
Ilfracombe Devon 3 V15
Ilkeston Derby 11 S21
Ilkley W Yorks 15 Q20
Illogan Cornw'l 2 X13
Ilminster Som'set 4 W18
Immingham NE Lincs 17 Q23
Inagh Clare 38 S5
Inch Cork 38 U9
Inch Kerry 38 T4
Inchigeelagh Cork 38 U5
Inchnadamph H'land 27 E15
Inchture Perth/Kinr 25 K17
Ingatestone Essex 7 U24
Ingleton N Yorks 15 P19
Ingoldmells Lincs 12 R24
Ingram Northum 21 M20
Ingrave Essex 7 U24
Inishannon Cork 39 U6
Inishcrone Sligo 35 P5
Inishkeen Monaghan 37 P10
Inishrush
  Londonderry 33 N10
Inistioge Kilkenny 40 T9
Inkberrow Worcs 11 T20
Innellan Arg/Bute 18 L14
Innerleithen
  Scot Borders 20 L17
Innermessan
  Dumf/Gal 18 N14
Innfield Meath 37 R10
Insch Aberds 29 H18
Instow Devon 3 V15
Inver Donegal 32 N7
Inverallochy Aberds 29 G20
Inveran Galway 34 R5
Inveran H'land 28 G15
Inveraray Arg/Bute 23 K13
Inverarity Angus 25 J18
Inverbervie Aberds 25 J19
Invergarry H'land 24 H14
Invergordon H'land 28 G15
Invergowrie
  Dundee C 25 K17
Inverie H'land 23 H12
Inverinate H'land 23 H13
Inverkeilor Angus 25 J18
Inverkeithing Fife 24 K17
Inverkirkaig H'land 27 F13
Inverlochlarig Stirl 24 K14
Invermoriston H'land 24 H14
Inverness H'land 28 H15
Inversnaid Stirl 24 K14
Inverurie Aberds 29 H19
Ipswich Suffolk 13 T26
Irchester Northants 12 T22
Irlam Gtr Man 15 R19
Ironbridge Telford 10 S19
Irthlingborough
  Northants 12 T22
Irvine N Ayrs 19 L14
Irvinestown
  Fermanagh 32 P8
Islandtown Antrim 33 N11

Isle of Whithorn
Dumf/Gal 19 N15
Isleham Cambs 12 T24
Islington Gtr Lon 6 U23
Islip Oxon 5 U21
Ivinghoe Bucks 6 U22
Ivybridge Devon 3 X16
Iwerne Minster
Dorset 5 W19
Ixworth Suffolk 13 T25

J

Jamestown W Dunb 24 K14
Jarrow Tyne/Wear 21 N21
Jaywick Essex 7 U26
Jedburgh
Scot Borders 21 M18
Jervaulx N Yorks 16 P20
John o'Groats H'land 29 E17
Johnshaven Aberds 25 J19
Johnston Pembs 9 U13
Johnstone Renf 19 L15
Johnstown Bridge
Kildare 37 R10
Johnstown Kilkenny 39 S8
Juliustown Meath 37 Q11

K

Kames Arg/Bute 18 L13
Kanturk Cork 39 T6
Katesbridge Down 33 P11
Kea Cornw'l 2 X13
Keadow Roscommon 36 P7
Keady Armagh 33 P10
Kealkill Cork 38 U5
Kedington Suffolk 12 T24
Keel Mayo 34 Q3
Keelby Lincs 17 Q23
Keele Staffs 10 R19
Keenagh Longford 36 Q8
Kegworth Leics 11 S21
Keighley W Yorks 15 Q20
Keillmore Arg/Bute 18 L12
Keiss H'land 29 E17
Keith Moray 29 G18
Keld N Yorks 15 P17
Kellas Moray 28 G17
Kells Kilkenny 40 S9
Kells Meath 37 Q10
Kells Antrim 33 N11
Kellystown Louth 37 Q10
Kelsale Suffolk 13 T27
Kelsall Ches 10 R18
Kelso Scot Borders 21 L19
Keltneyburn
Perth/Kinr 24 J15
Kelty Fife 24 K17
Kelvedon Essex 7 U25
Kelynack Cornw'l 2 X12
Kemble Glos 5 U20
Kemnay Aberds 25 H19
Kempsey Worcs 10 T19
Kempston Beds 12 T22
Kendal Cumb 15 P18
Kenilworth Warwick 11 T20
Kenmare Kerry 38 U4
Kenmore Perth/Kinr 24 J16
Kennacraig Arg/Bute 18 L13
Kennethmont Aberds 29 H18
Kennford Devon 4 W16
Kenninghall Norfolk 13 T25
Kennington Oxon 5 U21
Kensington &
Chelsea Gtr Lon 6 U23
Kentford Suffolk 13 T25
Kentisbeare Devon 4 W17
Kentstown Meath 37 Q10
Kerry Powys 10 S17
Kerrysdale H'land 27 G12
Kershopefoot
Scot Borders 20 M18
Kesgrave Suffolk 13 T26
Kesh Fermanagh 32 N8
Keshcarrigan Leitrim 36 P8
Kessingland Suffolk 13 T27
Keswick Cumb 20 N17
Kettering Northants 12 T22
Kettlewell N Yorks 15 P19
Ketton Rutl'd 12 S22
Kexby Lincs 17 R22

Keyingham ER Yorks 17 Q23
Keymer W Sussex 6 W23
Keynsham
Bath/NE Som'set 4 V18
Keysoe Beds 12 T23
Keyworth Notts 11 S21
Kibworth Beauchamp
Leics 11 S22
Kidderminster Worcs 10 T19
Kidlington Oxon 5 U21
Kidsgrove Staffs 10 R19
Kidstones N Yorks 15 P19
Kidwelly Carms 9 U15
Kielder Northum 21 M18
Kilamery Kilkenny 40 T9
Kilbaha Clare 38 S4
Kilbeggan
Westmeath 36 R9
Kilbeheny Limerick 39 T7
Kilbennan Church
Galway 35 Q6
Kilberry Meath 37 Q10
Kilberry Arg/Bute 18 L12
Kilbirnie N Ayrs 19 L14
Kilbrickan Galway 34 R4
Kilbride Wicklow 40 S11
Kilbride Arg/Bute 23 K13
Kilbrien Waterford 39 T8
Kilbrittain Cork 39 U6
Kilcadzow S Lanarks 19 L16
Kilcar Donegal 32 N6
Kilchattan Arg/Bute 18 L13
Kilchenzie Arg/Bute 18 M12
Kilchiaran Arg/Bute 18 L11
Kilchoan H'land 22 J11
Kilchreest Galway 35 R6
Kilchrenan Arg/Bute 23 K13
Kilclooney Donegal 32 N7
Kilcock Kildare 37 R10
Kilcoe Cork 38 U5
Kilcogy Cavan 36 Q9
Kilcolgan Galway 35 R6
Kilconly Galway 35 Q6
Kilconnell Galway 35 R7
Kilcoo Down 33 P11
Kilcoole Wicklow 37 R11
Kilcormac Offaly 36 R8
Kilcornan Limerick 39 S6
Kilcreggan Arg/Bute 23 L14
Kilcrohane Cork 38 U4
Kilcullen Kildare 37 R10
Kilcurry Louth 37 P11
Kildalkey Meath 37 Q10
Kildare Kildare 37 R10
Kildavin Carlow 40 S10
Kildimo Limerick 39 S6
Kildonan H'land 28 F16
Kildorrery Cork 39 T7
Kilfane Kilkenny 40 S9
Kilfeakle Tipperary 39 T7
Kilfearagh Clare 38 S4
Kilfenora Clare 35 S5
Kilfinan Arg/Bute 18 L13
Kilfinnane Limerick 39 T7
Kilflynn Kerry 38 T4
Kilgarrif Galway 35 R5
Kilgarvan Kerry 38 U5
Kilglass Galway 35 R7
Kilglass Sligo 35 P5
Kilgobnet Kerry 38 T4
Kilgolagh Cavan 36 Q9
Kilham ER Yorks 17 P23
Kilkea Kildare 40 S10
Kilkee Clare 38 S4
Kilkeel Down 37 P11
Kilkelly Mayo 35 Q6
Kilkenny Kilkenny 40 S9
Kilkerrin Galway 35 Q6
Kilkhampton Cornw'l 2 W14
Kilkieran Galway 34 R4
Kilkinlea Kerry 38 T5
Kilkishen Clare 39 S6
Kill Kildare 37 R10
Kill Waterford 40 T9
Killadangan Mayo 34 Q4
Killadeas Fermanagh 32 P8
Killadoon Mayo 34 Q4
Killadysert Clare 38 S5
Killala Mayo 35 P5
Killaloe Tipperary 39 S7
Killaloo Londonderry 32 N9
Killamarsh Derby 16 R21
Killane Offaly 36 R9
Killarbran Fermanagh 32 P9
Killarga Leitrim 32 P7
Killargue Leitrim 36 P7
Killarney Kerry 38 T5
Killashandra Cavan 36 P8
Killashee Longford 36 Q8

Killavally Mayo 34 Q5
Killavullen Cork 39 T6
Killeagh Cork 39 U8
Killean Arg/Bute 18 L12
Killearn Stirl 24 K15
Killeen Tipperary 36 R8
Killeen Tyrone 33 N10
Killeevan Monaghan 36 P9
Killeglan
Roscommon 36 R7
Killeigh Offaly 36 R9
Killen Tyrone 32 N8
Killenagh Wexford 40 S11
Killenaule Tipperary 39 S8
Killerig Carlow 40 S10
Killeter Tyrone 32 N8
Killimor Galway 35 R7
Killin Stirl 24 K15
Killinaboy Clare 35 S5
Killinaspick Kilkenny 40 T9
Killiney Dublin 37 R11
Killinghall N Yorks 16 P20
Killinick Wexford 40 T11
Killorglin Kerry 38 T4
Killough Down 33 P12
Killowen Down 37 P11
Killsaran Louth 37 Q11
Killtullagh Galway 35 R6
Killucan Westmeath 36 Q9
Killurin Wexford 40 T10
Killybegs Donegal 32 N7
Killyfassy Cavan 36 Q9
Killygordon Donegal 32 N8
Killykergan
Londonderry 33 M10
Killylea Armagh 33 P10
Killyleagh Down 33 P12
Killyon Offaly 36 R8
Kilmacolm Invercl 19 L14
Kilmacow Kilkenny 40 T9
Kilmacrenan Donegal 32 M8
Kilmacthomas
Waterford 40 T9
Kilmaganny Kilkenny 40 T9
Kilmaine Mayo 35 Q5
Kilmaley Clare 38 S5
Kilmallock Limerick 39 T6
Kilmaluag H'land 26 G11
Kilmanagh Kilkenny 40 S9
Kilmany Fife 25 K18
Kilmarnock E Ayrs 19 L15
Kilmartin Arg/Bute 23 K13
Kilmaurs E Ayrs 19 L14
Kilmeadan Waterford 40 T9
Kilmeage Kildare 37 R10
Kilmeedy Limerick 39 T6
Kilmelford Arg/Bute 23 K13
Kilmichael Cork 38 U5
Kilmihil Clare 38 S5
Kilmore Wexford 40 T10
Kilmore Quay
Wexford 40 T10
Kilmory Arg/Bute 18 L12
Kilmory H'land 22 H11
Kilmory H'land 22 J11
Kilmuckridge
Wexford 40 S11
Kilmuir H'land 28 G15
Kilmurry Clare 38 S5
Kilmurry Clare 39 S6
Kilmurvy Clare 34 R4
Kilnaleck Cavan 36 Q9
Kilninver Arg/Bute 23 K12
Kilnsea ER Yorks 17 Q24
Kilpatrick Cork 39 U6
Kilrea Londonderry 33 N10
Kilreekil Galway 35 R7
Kilrenny Fife 25 K18
Kilronan Clare 34 R4
Kilronane Cork 38 U5
Kilross Tipperary 39 T7
Kilrush Clare 38 S5
Kilsallagh Galway 35 Q6
Kilsby Northants 11 T21
Kilshanny Clare 34 S5
Kilsheelan Tipperary 39 T8
Kilsyth N Lanarks 24 L15
Kiltamagh Mayo 35 Q5
Kiltartan Galway 35 R6
Kiltealy Wexford 40 S10
Kilteel Kildare 37 R10
Kilteely Limerick 39 S7
Kiltegan Wicklow 40 S10
Kiltiernan Dublin 37 R11
Kiltoom Roscommon 36 R7
Kiltormer Galway 35 R7
Kiltyclogher Leitrim 32 P7
Kilwinning N Ayrs 19 L14
Kilworth Cork 39 T7

Kimbolton Cambs 12 T23
Kimpton Herts 6 U23
Kinalag Galway 35 Q6
Kinawley Fermanagh 32 P8
Kinbrace H'land 28 F16
Kinbuck Stirl 24 K16
Kincardine Fife 24 K16
Kincardine H'land 28 G15
Kincaslough Donegal 32 M7
Kincraig H'land 24 H16
Kindrum Donegal 32 M8
Kineton Warwick 11 T20
Kingarrow Donegal 32 N7
Kingarth Arg/Bute 18 L13
Kinghorn Fife 25 K17
King's Cliffe
Northants 12 S23
Kings Langley Herts 6 U23
King's Lynn Norfolk 12 S24
King's Somborne
Hants 5 V21
King's Sutton
Northants 11 T21
King's Thorn Heref'd 10 U18
King's Worthy Hants 5 V21
Kingsbarns Fife 25 K18
Kingsbridge Devon 3 X16
Kingsbury Warwick 11 S20
Kingsclere Hants 5 V21
Kingscourt Cavan 37 Q10
Kingsdown Kent 7 V26
Kingskerswell Devon 3 X16
Kingsland Heref'd 10 T18
Kingsley Hants 6 V22
Kingsley Staffs 11 R20
Kingsteignton Devon 4 W16
Kingston Bagpuize
Oxon 5 U21
Kingston Devon 3 X16
Kingston Gtr Lon 6 U23
Kingston Upon Hull
Kingston/Hull 17 Q23
Kingswear Devon 3 X16
Kingswood S Glos 4 V18
Kington Heref'd 10 T17
Kingussie H'land 24 H15
Kinloch Rannoch
Perth/Kinr 24 J15
Kinloch H'land 22 H11
Kinloch H'land 27 F14
Kinlochbervie H'land 27 F13
Kinloch H'land 23 J13
Kinlochewe H'land 27 G13
Kinlochleven H'land 23 J14
Kinlochmoidart
H'land 23 J12
Kinloss Moray 28 G16
Kinlough Leitrim 32 P7
Kinmel Bay Conwy 8 R16
Kinnegad Westmeath 36 R9
Kinnitty Offaly 36 R8
Kinross Perth/Kinr 24 K17
Kinsale Cork 39 U6
Kintarvie W Isles 26 F7
Kintore Aberds 25 H19
Kinuachdrachd
Arg/Bute 23 K12
Kinvarra Galway 35 R6
Kinver Staffs 10 T19
Kippax W Yorks 16 Q21
Kippen Stirl 24 K15
Kircubbin Down 33 P12
Kirk Michael I/Man 14 P14
Kirkbean Dumf/Gal 20 N16
Kirkbride Cumb 20 N17
Kirkburton W Yorks 16 Q20
Kirkby Lonsdale
Cumb 15 P18
Kirkby Malzeard
N Yorks 16 P20
Kirkby Stephen
Cumb 15 P19
Kirkby Thore Cumb 21 N18
Kirkby Mersey 15 R18
Kirkby-in-Ashfield
Notts 11 R21
Kirkby-in-Furness
Cumb 15 P17
Kirkbymoorside
N Yorks 17 P22
Kirkcaldy Fife 25 K17
Kirkcolm Dumf/Gal 18 N13
Kirkconnel Dumf/Gal 19 M15
Kirkcowan Dumf/Gal 19 N14
Kirkcudbright
Dumf/Gal 19 N15
Kirkham Lancs 15 Q18
Kirkinner Dumf/Gal 19 N15
Kirkintilloch E Dunb 19 L15

Kirkland Dumf/Gal 19 M16
Kirkliston C/Edinb 24 L17
Kirkmichael
Perth/Kinr 24 J16
Kirkmichael S Ayrs 19 M14
Kirknewton Northum 21 L19
Kirkoswald Cumb 21 N18
Kirkoswald S Ayrs 18 M14
Kirkpatrick Durham
Dumf/Gal 19 M16
Kirkpatrick Fleming
Dumf/Gal 20 M17
Kirkton of Glenisla
Angus 24 J17
Kirkton of Largo Fife 25 K18
Kirkwhelpington
Northum 21 M20
Kirriemuir Angus 25 J18
Kirtling Cambs 12 T24
Kirtlington Oxon 11 U21
Kirton in Lindsey
N Lincs 17 R22
Kirton Lincs 12 S23
Kishkeam Cork 38 T5
Knaresborough
N Yorks 16 P21
Knayton N Yorks 16 P21
Knebworth Herts 6 U23
Knighton Powys 10 T17
Knock Clare 38 S5
Knock Mayo 35 Q6
Knockaderry
Limerick 39 T6
Knockagree Cork 38 T5
Knockalina Mayo 34 P4
Knockalough Clare 38 S5
Knockananna
Wicklow 40 S11
Knockatallan
Monaghan 32 P9
Knockbrit Tipperary 39 T8
Knockcroghery
Roscommon 36 Q7
Knockfold Donegal 32 M7
Knocklofty Tipperary 39 T8
Knocklong Limerick 39 T7
Knocktopher
Kilkenny 40 T9
Knott End-on-Sea
Lancs 15 Q18
Knottingley W Yorks 16 Q21
Knowle W Midlands 11 T20
Knowsley Mersey 15 R18
Knutsford Ches 15 R19
Kyle of Lochalsh
H'land 27 H12
Kyleakin H'land 27 H12
Kylerhea H'land 23 H12
Kylesa Galway 34 R4
Kylestrome H'land 27 F13

L

Laban Galway 35 R6
Labasheeda Clare 38 S5
Labby Londonderry 33 N10
Laceby NE Lincs 17 Q23
Lack Fermanagh 32 N8
Lackamore Tipperary 39 S7
Lacock Wilts 5 V19
Ladock Cornw'l 2 X14
Ladybank Fife 25 K17
Ladysbridge Cork 39 U7
Lagg Arg/Bute 18 L12
Laggan H'land 24 H14
Laggan H'land 24 H15
Laggan Moray 29 H17
Laghtgeorge Galway 35 R6
Laghy Donegal 32 N7
Lahard Cavan 36 Q8
Lahardaun Mayo 34 P5
Laide H'land 27 G12
Lairg H'land 28 F15
Lakenheath Suffolk 13 T25
Lakyle Clare 38 S5
Lamberhurst Kent 7 V24
Lambeth Gtr Lon 6 V23
Lambley Northum 21 N18
Lambourn W Berks 5 U20
Lamlash N Ayrs 18 L13
Lampeter Ceredig'n 9 T15
Lanark S Lanarks 19 L16
Lancaster Lancs 15 P18
Lancheston Durham 21 N20
Lancing W Sussex 6 W23
Landkey Devon 3 V15

Landrake *Cornw'l* 3 X15
Lanesborough
  Longford 36 Q8
Langford Budville
  Som'set 4 W17
Langham *Rutl'd* 11 S22
Langholm *Dumf/Gal* 20 M18
Langport *Som'set* 4 V18
Langsett *S Yorks* 16 Q20
Langtoft *ER Yorks* 17 P23
Langtoft *Lincs* 12 S23
Langton Matravers
  Dorset 5 W19
Langtree *Devon* 3 W15
Langwathby *Cumb* 21 N18
Langwell *H'land* 28 F15
Lanivet *Cornw'l* 2 X14
Lapford *Devon* 3 W16
Laracor *Meath* 37 Q10
Laragh *Wicklow* 40 R11
Larbert *Falk* 24 K16
Largan *Mayo* 34 P4
Largs *N Ayrs* 18 L14
Largy *Donegal* 32 N6
Larkhall *S Lanarks* 19 L16
Larkhill *Wilts* 5 V20
Larne *Antrim* 33 N12
Lasswade *Midloth* 20 L17
Latchingdon *Essex* 7 U25
Latheron *H'land* 28 F17
Lattin *Tipperary* 39 T7
Lauder *Scot Borders* 21 L18
Laugharne *Carms* 9 U15
Launceston *Cornw'l* 3 W15
Lauragh *Kerry* 38 U4
Laurencekirk *Aberds* 25 J19
Laurencetown
  Galway 36 R7
Laurieston *Dumf/Gal* 19 N15
Lavendon *M/Keynes* 12 T22
Lavenham *Suffolk* 13 T25
Lavey *Cavan* 36 Q9
Lawers *Perth/Kinr* 24 J15
Lawrencetown *Down* 33 P11
Laxey *I/Man* 14 P15
Laxfield *Suffolk* 13 T26
Laxford Bridge
  H'land 27 F13
Laxton *Notts* 11 R22
Layer de la Haye
  Essex 7 U25
Laytown *Meath* 37 Q11
Lazonby *Cumb* 21 N18
Lea *Lincs* 17 R22
Leadburn *Midloth* 20 L17
Leaden Roding
  Essex 7 U24
Leadenham *Lincs* 12 R22
Leadgate *Durham* 21 N20
Leadhills *S Lanarks* 19 M16
Leap *Cork* 38 U5
Leasingham *Lincs* 12 R23
Leatherhead *Surrey* 6 V23
Lechlade *Glos* 5 U20
Leckanarainey
  Leitrim 32 P7
Leckaun *Leitrim* 32 P7
Leckemy *Donegal* 33 M9
Ledbury *Heref'd* 10 T19
Ledmore *H'land* 27 F14
Leeds *W Yorks* 16 Q20
Leedstown *Cornw'l* 2 X13
Leek *Staffs* 10 R19
Leeming Bar *N Yorks* 16 P20
Leenaun *Galway* 34 Q4
Lee-on-the-Solent
  Hants 5 W21
Legbourne *Lincs* 17 R24
Legoniel *Antrim* 33 N12
Lehinch *Clare* 34 S5
Leicester *Leics C* 11 S21
Leigh *Gtr Man* 15 Q18
Leigh *Worcs* 10 T19
Leighlinbridge *Carlow* 40 S10
Leighton Buzzard
  Beds 12 U22
Leintwardine *Heref'd* 10 T18
Leiston *Suffolk* 13 T27
Leith *C/Edin* 25 L17
Leitholm
  Scot Borders 21 L19
Leitrim *Leitrim* 36 Q7
Leixlip *Kildare* 37 R11
Lelant *Cornw'l* 2 X13
Lenham *Kent* 7 V25
Lennoxtown *E Dunb* 24 L15

Leominster *Heref'd* 10 T18
Lephin *H'land* 26 H10
Lerrig *Kerry* 38 T4
Lesbury *Northum* 21 M20
Leslie *Fife* 25 K17
Lesmahagow
  S Lanarks 19 L16
Leswalt *Dumf/Gal* 18 N13
Letchworth *Herts* 12 U23
Letterbreen
  Fermanagh 32 P8
Letterfrack *Galway* 34 Q4
Letterkenny *Donegal* 32 N8
Lettermacaward
  Donegal 32 N7
Lettermore *Galway* 34 R4
Lettermullan *Galway* 34 R4
Letterston *Pembs* 9 U14
Lettoch *H'land* 28 H17
Leuchars *Fife* 25 K18
Leumrabhagh
  W Isles 26 F11
Leven *ER Yorks* 17 Q23
Leven *Fife* 25 K18
Lewes *E Sussex* 6 W24
Lewisham *Gtr Lon* 6 V23
Lewiston *H'land* 28 H15
Leyburn *N Yorks* 15 P20
Leyland *Lancs* 15 Q18
Leysdown on Sea
  Kent 7 V25
Lhanbryde *Moray* 29 G17
Liatrie *H'land* 27 H14
Lichfield *Staffs* 11 S20
Lidgate *Suffolk* 13 T25
Lifford *Donegal* 32 N9
Lifton *Devon* 3 W15
Ligfordrum *Tyrone* 32 N9
Lilleshall *Telford* 10 S19
Limavady
  Londonderry 33 M10
Limerick *Limerick* 39 S6
Limerick Junction
  Tipperary 39 T7
Lincoln *Lincs* 17 R22
Lindale *Cumb* 15 P18
Lingfield *Surrey* 6 V23
Linkinhorne *Cornw'l* 3 W15
Linlithgow *W Loth* 24 L16
Linslade *Beds* 12 U22
Linton *Cambs* 12 T24
Liphook *Hants* 6 V22
Lisacul *Roscommon* 35 Q6
Lisbane *Down* 33 N12
Lisbellaw *Fermanagh* 32 P8
Lisburn *Antrim* 33 N11
Liscannor *Clare* 34 S5
Liscarroll *Cork* 39 T6
Lisdoonvarna *Clare* 34 R5
Lisgall *Monaghan* 37 P10
Lisgarode *Tipperary* 39 S7
Lisheen *Clare* 38 S5
Liskeard *Cornw'l* 3 X15
Lislap *Tyrone* 32 N9
Lislea *Armagh* 37 P11
Lismore *Waterford* 39 T8
Lisnacree *Down* 37 P11
Lisnagry *Limerick* 39 S6
Lisnamusk
  Londonderry 33 N10
Lisnarrick *Fermanagh* 32 P8
Lisnaskea
  Fermanagh 32 P9
Lisnaveane
  Monaghan 36 P9
Lispole *Kerry* 38 T3
Lisronagh *Tipperary* 39 T8
Liss *Hants* 6 V22
Lissatintig Bridge
  Kerry 38 U4
Lisselton *Kerry* 38 T4
Lissett *ER Yorks* 17 P23
Lissinagroagh *Leitrim* 32 P7
Lissycasey *Clare* 38 S5
Listerlin *Kilkenny* 40 T9
Listowel *Kerry* 38 T5
Litcham *Norfolk* 13 S25
Litherland *Mersey* 15 R18
Little Shelford
  Cambs 12 T24
Little Stukeley
  Cambs 12 T23
Little Walsingham
  Norfolk 13 S25
Littleborough
  Gtr Man 15 Q19
Littlehampton
  W Sussex 6 W22
Littlemill *H'land* 28 G16

Littleport *Cambs* 12 T24
Littlestone-on-Sea
  Kent 7 W25
Littleton *Tipperary* 39 S8
Liverpool *Mersey* 15 R18
Livingston *W Loth* 24 L17
Lixnaw *Kerry* 38 T4
Lizard *Cornw'l* 2 Y13
Llanaber *Gwyn* 8 S15
Llanaelhaiarn *Gwyn* 8 S15
Llanafan-fawr *Powys* 9 T16
Llanarmon Dyffryn
  Ceiriog *Wrex* 10 S17
Llanarmon *Denbs* 10 R17
Llanarth *Ceredig'n* 9 T15
Llanarthney *Carms* 9 U15
Llanbadarn Fynydd
  Powys 9 T17
Llanbedr *Gwyn* 8 S15
Llanbedrog *Gwyn* 8 S15
Llanberis *Gwyn* 8 R15
Llanbister *Powys* 9 T17
Llanbrynmair *Powys* 8 S16
Llanddewi-Brefi
  Ceredig'n 9 T16
Llanddulas *Conwy* 8 R16
Llandeilo *Carms* 9 U16
Llandinam *Powys* 8 T17
Llandissilio *Pembs* 9 U14
Llandogo
  Monmouths 4 U18
Llandovery *Carms* 9 U16
Llandrillo *Denbs* 8 S17
Llandrindod Wells
  Powys 9 T17
Llandudno *Conwy* 8 R16
Llandybie *Carms* 9 U15
Llandyfriog *Ceredig'n* 9 T15
Llandygwydd
  Ceredig'n 9 T14
Llandyrnog *Denbs* 8 R17
Llandysul *Ceredig'n* 9 T15
Llanelidan *Denbs* 8 R17
Llanelli *Carms* 9 U15
Llanelltyd *Gwyn* 8 S16
Llaneneddwyn *Gwyn* 8 S15
Llanerchymedd *Angl* 8 R15
Llanerfyl *Powys* 8 S17
Llanfaethlu *Angl* 8 R14
Llanfair Caereinion
  Powys 8 S17
Llanfair Talhaiarn
  Conwy 8 R16
Llanfairfechan *Conwy* 8 R16
Llanfairpwllgwngyll
  Angl 8 R15
Llanfechain *Powys* 10 S17
Llanfechell *Angl* 8 R15
Llanfihangel-ar-arth
  Carms 9 T15
Llanfrynach *Powys* 9 U17
Llanfyllin *Powys* 10 S17
Llangadfan *Powys* 8 S17
Llangadog *Carms* 9 U16
Llangammarch Wells
  Powys 9 T16
Llangefni *Angl* 8 R15
Llangeitho *Ceredig'n* 9 T15
Llangelynin *Gwyn* 8 S15
Llangennech *Carms* 9 U15
Llangernyw *Conwy* 8 R16
Llangoed *Angl* 8 R15
Llangollen *Denbs* 10 S17
Llangorse *Powys* 9 U17
Llangranog *Ceredig'n* 9 T15
Llangunllo *Powys* 10 T17
Llangurig *Powys* 9 T16
Llangwm *Conwy* 8 R16
Llangwm *Monmouths* 4 U18
Llangybi *Ceredig'n* 9 T15
Llangynidr *Powys* 10 U17
Llangynog *Powys* 8 S17
Llanharan
  Rh Cyn Taff 4 U17
Llanidloes *Powys* 9 T16
Llanilar *Ceredig'n* 9 T15
Llanllyfni *Gwyn* 8 R15
Llannor *Gwyn* 8 S15
Llanon *Ceredig'n* 9 T15
Llanpumsaint *Carms* 9 U15
Llanrhaeadr-ym-
  Mochnant *Powys* 8 S17
Llanrhian *Pembs* 9 U13
Llanrhidian *Swan* 9 U15
Llanrhystyd
  Ceredig'n 9 T15
Llanrug *Gwyn* 8 R15
Llanrwst *Conwy* 8 R16
Llansannan *Conwy* 8 R16

Llansawel *Carms* 9 T15
Llanstephan *Carms* 9 U15
Llanthony
  Monmouths 10 U17
Llantrisant
  Rh Cyn Taff 4 U17
Llantwit-Major
  V/Glam 4 V17
Llanuwchllyn *Gwyn* 8 S16
Llanvihangel
  Crucorney
  Monmouths 10 U18
Llanwddyn *Powys* 8 S17
Llanwenog *Ceredig'n* 9 T15
Llanwrda *Carms* 9 U16
Llanwrtyd Wells
  Powys 9 T16
Llanyblodwel *Shrops* 10 S17
Llanybydder *Carms* 9 T15
Llanymynech *Powys* 10 S17
Llanystumdwy *Gwyn* 8 S15
Llay *Wrex* 10 R17
Lledrod *Ceredig'n* 9 T16
Llithfaen *Gwyn* 8 S15
Llwyngwril *Gwyn* 8 S15
Llyswen *Powys* 9 T17
Loanhead *Midloth* 20 L17
Lobinstown *Meath* 37 Q10
Loch Baghasdail
  W Isles 22 H9
Loch nam Madadh
  W Isles 26 G9
Lochailort *H'land* 23 J12
Lochaline *H'land* 23 J12
Lochans *Dumf/Gal* 18 N13
Locharbriggs
  Dumf/Gal 20 M16
Lochbuie *Arg/Bute* 23 K12
Lochcarron *H'land* 27 H12
Lochdon *Arg/Bute* 23 K12
Lochearnhead *Stirl* 24 K15
Lochgair *Arg/Bute* 23 K13
Lochgelly *Fife* 24 K17
Lochgilphead
  Arg/Bute 23 K13
Lochgoilhead
  Arg/Bute 23 K14
Lochinver *H'land* 27 F13
Lochmaben
  Dumf/Gal 20 M17
Lochranza *N Ayrs* 18 L13
Lochwinnoch *Renf* 19 L14
Lockerbie *Dumf/Gal* 20 M17
Lockton *N Yorks* 17 P22
Loddiswell *Devon* 3 X16
Loddon *Norfolk* 13 S27
Loftus
  Redcar/Clevel'd 17 N22
Logan *E Ayrs* 19 M15
Loghill *Limerick* 38 S5
London Colney *Herts* 6 U23
London *Gtr Lon* 6 U23
Long Ashton *Bristol* 4 V18
Long Bennington
  Lincs 11 S22
Long Clawson *Leics* 11 S22
Long Compton
  Warwick 11 T20
Long Crendon *Bucks* 6 U22
Long Eaton *Derby* 11 S21
Long Itchington
  Warwick 11 T21
Long Melford *Suffolk* 13 T25
Long Preston
  N Yorks 15 P19
Long Stratton *Norfolk* 13 T26
Long Sutton *Lincs* 12 S24
Longbenton
  Tyne/Wear 21 M20
Longbridge Deverill
  Wilts 5 V19
Longdon *Worcs* 10 T19
Longford *Longford* 36 Q8
Longford *Glos* 10 U19
Longforgan
  Perth/Kinr 25 K17
Longformacus
  Scot Borders 21 L19
Longframlington
  Northum 21 M20
Longhorsley *Northum* 21 M20
Longhoughton
  Northum 21 M20
Longnor *Staffs* 11 R20
Longridge *Lancs* 15 Q18
Longside *Aberds* 29 G20
Longton *Lancs* 15 Q18
Longtown *Cumb* 20 M18
Longtown *Heref'd* 10 U18

Longwood *Meath* 37 R10
Loose *Kent* 7 V25
Lossiemouth *Moray* 28 G17
Lostock Gralam
  Ches 15 R19
Lostwithiel *Cornw'l* 2 X14
Loughall *Armagh* 33 P10
Loughanavally
  Westmeath 36 R8
Loughanure *Donegal* 32 N7
Loughborough *Leics* 11 S21
Loughbrickland
  Down 33 P11
Loughglinn
  Roscommon 35 Q6
Loughguile *Antrim* 33 M11
Loughmoe *Tipperary* 39 S8
Loughor *Swan* 9 U15
Loughran *Antrim* 33 M11
Loughrea *Galway* 35 R6
Loughton *Essex* 6 U24
Louisburgh *Mayo* 34 Q4
Louth *Louth* 37 Q10
Louth *Lincs* 17 R23
Lowdham *Notts* 11 R22
Lower Beeding
  W Sussex 6 V23
Lower Killeyan
  Arg/Bute 18 L11
Lower Langford
  N Som'set 4 V18
Lower Mayland
  Essex 7 U25
Lower Shiplake *Oxon* 6 U22
Lowestoft *Suffolk* 13 T27
Lowick *Northum* 21 L20
Loxwood *W Sussex* 6 V22
Lubcroy *H'land* 27 G14
Lucan *Dublin* 37 R11
Lucker *Northum* 21 L20
Ludborough *Lincs* 17 R23
Ludford *Lincs* 17 R23
Ludgershall *Wilts* 5 V20
Ludgvan *Cornw'l* 2 X12
Ludham *Norfolk* 13 S27
Ludlow *Shrops* 10 T18
Lugatemple *Mayo* 35 Q5
Lugton *E Ayrs* 19 L14
Lugwardine *Heref'd* 10 T18
Lukeswell *Kilkenny* 40 T9
Lumphanan *Aberds* 29 H18
Lumsden *Aberds* 29 H18
Lurgan *Armagh* 33 P11
Lurgangreen *Louth* 37 Q11
Lusk *Dublin* 37 Q11
Luss *Arg/Bute* 24 K14
Lusta *H'land* 26 G10
Luton *Luton* 6 U23
Lutterworth *Leics* 11 T21
Lutton *Northants* 12 T23
Lybster *H'land* 28 F17
Lydd *Kent* 7 W25
Lydford *Devon* 3 W15
Lydham *Shrops* 10 S18
Lydney *Glos* 4 U18
Lyme Regis *Dorset* 4 W18
Lyminge *Kent* 7 V26
Lymington *Hants* 5 W20
Lymm *Warrington* 15 R19
Lympne *Kent* 7 V26
Lympstone *Devon* 4 W17
Lyndhurst *Hants* 5 W20
Lyneham *Wilts* 5 U20
Lynmouth *Devon* 3 V16
Lynton *Devon* 3 V16
Lyracrumpane *Kerry* 38 T5
Lytchett Minster
  Dorset 5 W19
Lytham St. Anne's
  Lancs 15 Q17
Lythe *N Yorks* 17 N22

M

Maam Cross *Galway* 34 R4
Maas *Donegal* 32 N7
Mablethorpe *Lincs* 17 R24
Macclesfield *Ches* 15 R19
Macduff *Aberds* 29 G18
Machen *Caerph* 4 U17
Machrihanish
  Arg/Bute 18 M12
Machynlleth *Powys* 8 S16
Mackan *Fermanagh* 32 P8
Macmerry *E Loth* 25 L18
Macosquin
  Londonderry 33 M10

Place	Area	Page	Grid
Macroom	Cork	39	U6
Madeley	Staffs	10	S19
Madley	Heref'd	10	T18
Maentwrog	Gwyn	8	S16
Maesteg	Bridg	9	U16
Maghera Londonderry		33	N10
Magherafelt Londonderry		33	N10
Magheragall	Antrim	33	N11
Magheraveely Fermanagh		32	P9
Maghery	Donegal	32	N7
Maghery	Armagh	33	N11
Maghull	Mersey	15	Q18
Magor	Monmouths	4	U18
Maguiresbridge Fermanagh		32	P9
Maiden Bradley	Wilts	5	V19
Maiden Newton Dorset		4	W18
Maidenhead	Windsor	6	U22
Maidstone	Kent	7	V25
Malahide	Dublin	37	R11
Maldon	Essex	7	U25
Malham	N Yorks	15	P19
Malin	Donegal	32	M9
Malin More	Donegal	32	N6
Mallaig	H'land	23	H12
Mallaranny	Mayo	34	Q4
Mallow	Cork	39	T6
Mallwyd	Gwyn	8	S16
Malmesbury	Wilts	5	U19
Malpas	Ches	10	R18
Maltby le Marsh Lincs		17	R24
Maltby	S Yorks	16	R21
Malton	N Yorks	17	P22
Manafon	Powys	8	S17
Manby	Lincs	17	R24
Manchester	Gtr Man	15	R19
Manea	Cambs	12	T24
Manfieldstown	Louth	37	Q11
Mangotsfield	S Glos	5	V19
Manningtree	Essex	13	U26
Manorbier	Pembs	9	U14
Manorhamilton Leitrim		32	P7
Manselstown Tipperary		39	S8
Mansfield	Notts	11	R21
Mansfield Woodhouse	Notts	11	R21
Manton	Rutl'd	12	S22
Manulla	Mayo	35	Q5
Marazion	Cornw'l	2	X13
March	Cambs	12	T24
Marden	Heref'd	10	T18
Marden	Kent	7	V24
Mareham le Fen Lincs		12	R23
Maresfield	E Sussex	6	W24
Marfleet Kingston/Hull		17	Q23
Margam Neath P Talb		9	U16
Margate	Kent	7	V26
Marham	Norfolk	13	S25
Market Bosworth Leics		11	S21
Market Deeping Lincs		12	S23
Market Drayton Shrops		10	S19
Market Harborough Leics		11	T22
Market Lavington Wilts		5	V20
Market Rasen	Lincs	17	R23
Market Warsop	Notts	11	R21
Market Weighton ER Yorks		17	Q22
Markethill	Armagh	33	P10
Markfield	Leics	11	S21
Markinch	Fife	25	K17
Marks Tey	Essex	7	U25
Markyate	Herts	6	U23
Marlborough	Devon	3	X16
Marlborough	Wilts	5	V20
Marlow	Bucks	6	U22
Marnhull	Dorset	5	W19
Marple	Gtr Man	15	R19
Marshchapel	Lincs	17	R24
Marshfield	S Glos	5	V19
Marske by the Sea Redcar/Clevel'd		16	N21
Marston Magna Som'set		4	W18
Martham	Norfolk	13	S27
Martin	Hants	5	W20
Martley	Worcs	10	T19
Martock	Som'set	4	W18
Marton	Lincs	17	R22
Marykirk	Aberds	25	J18
Maryport	Cumb	20	N17
Marytavy	Devon	3	W15
Marywell	Aberds	25	H18
Marywell	Angus	25	J18
Masham	N Yorks	16	P20
Mathry	Pembs	9	U13
Matlock	Derby	11	R20
Mattishall	Norfolk	13	S26
Mauchline	E Ayrs	19	L15
Maud	Aberds	29	G19
Maughold	I/Man	14	P15
Maulyneill	Kerry	38	U4
Maum	Galway	34	Q4
Mawgan	Cornw'l	2	X13
Maxwellheugh Scot Borders		21	L19
Maybole	S Ayrs	19	M14
Mayfield	E Sussex	7	V24
Mayfield	Staffs	11	R20
Maylough	Galway	35	R6
Maynooth	Kildare	37	R10
Mayo Bridge	Down	33	P11
Mayo	Mayo	35	Q5
Mealabost	W Isles	26	F11
Mealsgate	Cumb	20	N17
Measham	Leics	11	S20
Medstead	Hants	6	V21
Meenaneary	Donegal	32	N6
Meidrim	Carms	9	U15
Meifod	Powys	10	S17
Meigh	Armagh	37	P11
Meigle	Perth/Kinr	25	J17
Melbourn	Cambs	12	T24
Melbourne	Derby	11	S21
Melksham	Wilts	5	V19
Mell	Louth	37	Q11
Mellon Charles H'land		27	G12
Mellor	Lancs	15	Q18
Melmerby	Cumb	21	N18
Melrose Scot Borders		21	L18
Melsonby	N Yorks	16	P20
Meltham	W Yorks	15	Q20
Melton Constable Norfolk		13	S26
Melton Mowbray Leics		11	S22
Melton	Suffolk	13	T26
Melvaig	H'land	27	G12
Melvich	H'land	28	E16
Menai Bridge	Angl	8	R15
Mendlesham	Suffolk	13	T26
Menlough	Galway	35	R5
Mennock	Dumf/Gal	19	M16
Menston	W Yorks	15	Q20
Menstrie	Clack	24	K16
Meonstoke	Hants	5	W21
Meopham	Kent	7	V24
Mere Brow	Lancs	15	Q18
Mere	Wilts	5	V19
Meriden	W Midlands	11	S20
Merriott	Som'set	4	W18
Merthyr Tydfil Merth Tyd		9	U17
Merton	Gtr Lon	6	V23
Meshaw	Devon	3	W16
Messingham	N Lincs	17	Q22
Metfield	Suffolk	13	T26
Metheringham	Lincs	12	R23
Methil	Fife	25	K17
Methlick	Aberds	29	G18
Methven	Perth/Kinr	24	K16
Methwold	Norfolk	13	S25
Mevagissey	Cornw'l	2	X14
Mexborough	S Yorks	16	R21
Mey	H'land	29	E17
Micheldever	Hants	5	V21
Michelmersh	Hants	5	V20
Mickleover	Derby C	11	S20
Mickleton	Durham	21	N19
Mickleton	Glos	11	T20
Mid Lavant W Sussex		6	W22
Middle Barton	Oxon	11	U21
Middleham	N Yorks	16	P20
Middlemarsh	Dorset	5	W19
Middlesbrough Middlesbro		21	N21
Middleton Cheney Northants		11	T21
Middleton in Teesdale	Durham	21	N19
Middleton on the Wolds	ER Yorks	17	Q22
Middleton	Arg/Bute	22	K10
Middleton	Gtr Man	15	Q19
Middleton	Norfolk	12	S24
Middleton-on-Sea W Sussex		6	W22
Middletown	Armagh	33	P10
Middlewich	Ches	10	R19
Middlezoy	Som'set	4	V18
Midhurst	W Sussex	6	W22
Midleton	Cork	39	U7
Midsomer Norton Bath/NE Som'set		5	V19
Milborne Port Som'set		5	W19
Mildenhall	Suffolk	13	T25
Milestone	Tipperary	39	S7
Milford Haven	Pembs	9	U13
Milford	Cork	39	T6
Milford	Donegal	32	M8
Milford on Sea	Hants	5	W20
Milford	Surrey	6	V22
Millbrook	Meath	36	Q9
Millbrook	Cornw'l	3	X15
Millford	Armagh	33	P10
Millisle	Down	33	N12
Millom	Cumb	14	P17
Millport	N Ayrs	18	L14
Millstreet	Cork	38	T5
Millstreet	Waterford	39	T8
Milltown	Cavan	36	P9
Milltown	Galway	35	Q6
Milltown	Kerry	38	T3
Milltown	Kerry	38	T4
Milltown	Monaghan	33	P10
Milltown Malbay Clare		38	S5
Milltown	Antrim	33	N12
Milltown	Londonderry	33	M10
Milnathort	Perth/Kinr	24	K17
Milngavie	E Dunb	19	L15
Milnthorpe	Cumb	15	P18
Milovaig	H'land	26	H10
Milton Abbot	Devon	3	W15
Milton Keynes M/Keynes		12	T22
Milton	H'land	27	G14
Miltown	Kildare	37	R10
Milverton	Som'set	4	V17
Minane Bridge	Cork	39	U7
Minchinhampton Glos		5	U19
Minehead	Som'set	4	V17
Minera	Wrex	10	R17
Minety	Wilts	5	U20
Mingary	H'land	22	J11
Minnigaff	Dumf/Gal	19	N15
Minstead	Hants	5	W20
Minster	Kent	7	V25
Minster	Kent	7	V26
Minsterley	Shrops	10	S18
Mintlaw	Aberds	29	G19
Mirfield	W Yorks	16	Q20
Misterton	Notts	17	R22
Misterton	Som'set	4	W18
Mistley	Essex	13	U26
Mitchel Troy Monmouths		4	U18
Mitcheldean	Glos	5	U19
Mitchelstown	Cork	39	T7
Moate	Westmeath	36	R8
Modbury	Devon	3	X16
Modreeny	Tipperary	36	S7
Moelfre	Angl	8	R15
Moffat	Dumf/Gal	20	M17
Mohill	Leitrim	36	Q8
Moira	Down	33	P11
Mold	Flints	10	R17
Monaghan Monaghan		33	P10
Monar Lodge	H'land	27	H14
Monasterevin	Kildare	36	R9
Moneygall	Offaly	39	S8
Moneyglass	Antrim	33	N11
Moneymore Londonderry		33	N10
Moneyneany Londonderry		33	N10
Moniaive	Dumf/Gal	19	M16
Monifieth	Angus	25	K18
Monikie	Angus	25	J18
Monivea	Galway	35	R6
Monkland	Heref'd	10	T18
Monkokehampton Devon		3	W15
Monkstown	Cork	39	U7
Monkton	S Ayrs	19	L14
Monmouth Monmouths		4	U18
Montacute	Som'set	4	W18
Montgomery	Powys	10	S17
Montrose	Angus	25	J19
Monymusk	Aberds	25	H18
Mooncoin	Kilkenny	40	T9
Moone	Kildare	40	S10
Moorfields	Antrim	33	N11
Morar	H'land	23	J12
Morchard Bishop Devon		4	W16
Mordiford	Heref'd	10	T18
Morebattle Scot Borders		21	L19
Morecambe	Lancs	15	P18
Moretonhampstead Devon		3	W16
Moreton-in-Marsh Glos		11	U20
Morley	W Yorks	16	Q20
Mornington	Meath	37	Q11
Morpeth	Northum	21	M20
Mortehoe	Devon	3	V15
Mortimer's Cross Heref'd		10	T18
Morwenstow	Cornw'l	2	W14
Mossley	Antrim	33	N12
Mossley	Gtr Man	15	Q19
Moss-side	Antrim	33	M11
Mostyn	Flints	15	R17
Motcombe	Dorset	5	V19
Motherwell N Lanarks		19	L16
Mottisfont	Hants	5	V20
Moulton	Lincs	12	S23
Moulton	Northants	11	T22
Moulton	Suffolk	13	T25
Mount Bellew Bridge Galway		35	R7
Mount Ida	Down	33	P11
Mount Nugent	Cavan	36	Q9
Mount Talbot Roscommon		35	Q7
Mountain Ash Rh Cyn Taff		9	U17
Mountcharles Donegal		32	N7
Mountfield	Tyrone	32	N9
Mountjoy	Tyrone	32	N9
Mountmellick	Laois	36	R9
Mountnorris	Armagh	33	P11
Mountrath	Laois	40	R9
Mountshannon	Clare	35	S7
Mountsorrel	Leics	11	S21
Mousehole	Cornw'l	2	X12
Mouswald	Dumf/Gal	20	M17
Moville	Donegal	33	M9
Moy	H'land	28	H15
Moy	Tyrone	33	P10
Moyad	Down	37	P11
Moyard	Galway	34	Q3
Moyasta	Clare	38	S4
Moycullen	Galway	35	R5
Moymore	Clare	39	S6
Moynalty	Meath	37	Q10
Moyne	Longford	36	Q8
Moyne	Tipperary	39	S8
Moyroughly Westmeath		36	R8
Moyvally	Kildare	37	R10
Moyvore	Westmeath	36	Q8
Much Dewchurch Heref'd		10	U18
Much Marcle	Heref'd	10	U19
Much Wenlock Shrops		10	S18
Muchalls	Aberds	25	H19
Muckross	Kerry	38	T5
Muff	Donegal	32	M9
Muine Bheag	Carlow	40	S10
Muineagh	Donegal	32	M8
Muir of Ord	H'land	28	G15
Muirdrum	Angus	25	J18
Muirhead	N Lanarks	19	L15
Muirkirk	E Ayrs	19	L15
Muker	N Yorks	15	P19
Mulben	Moray	29	G17
Mullagh	Cavan	37	Q10
Mullagh	Galway	35	R7
Mullagh	Meath	37	R10
Mullaghnaneane Sligo		32	P6
Mullan	Fermanagh	32	P8
Mullans Town	Tyrone	33	N9
Mullanys Cross	Sligo	35	P6
Mullarts	Antrim	33	M11
Mulldonagh Londonderry		32	N9
Mullinahone Tipperary		39	S8
Mullinavat	Kilkenny	40	T9
Mullingar	Westmeath	36	Q9
Mullion	Cornw'l	2	X13
Mullughmore	Sligo	32	P7
Mundesley	Norfolk	13	S26
Mundford	Norfolk	13	S25
Mungret	Limerick	39	S6
Munlochy	H'land	28	G15
Murlaggan	H'land	23	J13
Murroogh	Clare	34	R5
Murton	Durham	21	N21
Musbury	Devon	4	W17
Musselburgh	E Loth	25	L17
Muthill	Perth/Kinr	24	K16
Mybster	H'land	28	F17
Myddfai	Carms	9	U16
Myddle	Shrops	10	S18
Mydroilyn	Ceredig'n	9	T15
Mynydd Isa	Flints	10	R17
Myshall	Carlow	40	S10

N

Place	Area	Page	Grid
N. Queensferry	Fife	24	K17
Naas	Kildare	37	R10
Nad	Cork	39	T6
Nafferton	ER Yorks	17	P23
Nailsea	N Som'set	4	V18
Nailsworth	Glos	5	U19
Nairn	H'land	28	G16
Nannerch	Flints	14	R17
Nantwich	Ches	10	R18
Nappa	N Yorks	15	Q19
Naran	Donegal	32	N7
Narberth	Pembs	9	U14
Narborough	Leics	11	S21
Naseby	Northants	11	T22
Naul	Dublin	37	Q11
Navan	Meath	37	Q10
Navenby	Lincs	12	R22
Neale	Mayo	35	Q5
Neath	Neath P Talb	9	U16
Necton	Norfolk	13	S25
Needham Market Suffolk		13	T26
Needingworth Cambs		12	T23
Nefyn	Gwyn	8	S14
Neilston	E Renf	19	L15
Nelson	Lancs	15	Q19
Nenagh	Tipperary	39	S7
Nenthead	Cumb	21	N19
Neston	Ches	15	R17
Nether Stowey Som'set		4	V17
Netheravon	Wilts	5	V20
Netherbury	Dorset	4	W18
Netherton	Northum	21	M19
Nethy Bridge	H'land	28	H16
Netley	Hants	5	W21
Nettlebed	Oxon	6	U22
Nettleham	Lincs	17	R23
Nettleton	Lincs	17	R23
Nevern	Pembs	9	T14
New Abbey Dumf/Gal		20	N16
New Aberdour Aberds		29	G19
New Alresford	Hants	5	V21
New Birmingham Tipperary		39	S8
New Buckenham Norfolk		13	T26
New Buildings Londonderry		32	N9
New Chapel Cross Kerry		38	U3
New Clipstone	Notts	11	R21
New Costessey Norfolk		13	S26
New Cumnock E Ayrs		19	M15
New Deer	Aberds	29	G19
New Earswick C/York		16	Q21
New Edlington S Yorks		16	R21
New Galloway Dumf/Gal		19	M15
New Holland	N Lincs	17	Q23
New Inn	Cavan	36	Q9
New Inn	Galway	35	R7
New Inn	Laois	36	R9
New Luce	Dumf/Gal	18	N14
New Mills	Derby	15	R20
New Milton	Hants	5	W20

New Pitsligo *Aberds* 29 G19
New Quay *Ceredig'n* 9 T15
New Radnor *Powys* 10 T17
New Romney *Kent* 7 W25
New Ross *Wexford* 40 T10
New Rossington
S Yorks 16 R21
New Scone
Perth/Kinr 24 K17
New Tredegar
Caerph 4 U17
New Waltham
NE Lincs 17 Q23
Newark-on-Trent
Notts 11 R22
Newbiggin-by-the-
Sea *Northum* 21 M20
Newbigging
S Lanarks 20 L16
Newbliss *Monaghan* 36 P9
Newborough *Angl* 8 R15
Newbridge *Galway* 35 Q7
Newbridge *Kildare* 37 R10
Newbridge *Limerick* 39 S6
Newbridge on Wye
Powys 9 T17
Newbridge *Caerph* 4 U17
Newbrough *Northum* 21 M19
Newburgh *Aberds* 29 H19
Newburgh *Fife* 25 K17
Newburn *Tyne/Wear* 21 N20
Newbury *W Berks* 5 V21
Newby Bridge *Cumb* 15 P18
Newbyth *Aberds* 29 G19
Newcastle Emlyn
Carms 9 T15
Newcastle *Tipperary* 39 T8
Newcastle *Wicklow* 37 R11
Newcastle *Down* 33 P12
Newcastle *Shrops* 10 T17
Newcastle West
Limerick 38 T5
Newcastleton
Scot Borders 20 M18
Newcastle-Under-
Lyme *Staffs* 10 R19
Newcastle-Upon-
Tyne *Tyne/Wear* 21 N20
Newchurch *Powys* 10 T17
Newdigate *Surrey* 6 V23
Newent *Glos* 10 U19
Newgale *Pembs* 9 U13
Newham *Gtr Lon* 6 U24
Newhaven *E Sussex* 6 W24
Newick *E Sussex* 6 W24
Newington *Kent* 7 V25
Newington *Kent* 7 V26
Newinn *Tipperary* 39 T8
Newlyn East *Cornw'l* 2 X13
Newlyn *Cornw'l* 2 X12
Newmachar *Aberds* 29 H19
Newmarket *Cork* 39 T6
Newmarket *Suffolk* 12 T24
Newmarket *W Isles* 26 F11
Newmarket-on-
Fergus *Clare* 39 S6
Newmill *Moray* 29 G18
Newmills *Donegal* 32 N8
Newmilns *E Ayrs* 19 L15
Newnham *Glos* 5 U19
Newport *Mayo* 34 Q4
Newport *Tipperary* 39 S7
Newport Pagnell
M/Keynes 12 T22
Newport *Essex* 12 U24
Newport *I/Wight* 5 W21
Newport *Newp* 4 U18
Newport *Pembs* 9 T14
Newport *Telford* 10 S19
Newport-on-Tay *Fife* 25 K18
Newquay *Cornw'l* 2 X13
Newry *Down* 33 P11
Newton Abbot *Devon* 4 W16
Newton Arlosh *Cumb* 20 N17
Newton Aycliffe
Durham 21 N20
Newton Ferrers
Devon 3 X15
Newton le Willows
Mersey 15 R18
Newton Mearns
E Renf 19 L15
Newton Poppleford
Devon 4 W17
Newton St. Cyres
Devon 4 W16
Newton Stewart
Dumf/Gal 19 N15
Newton *Lancs* 15 Q19

Newtongrange
Midloth 20 L17
Newtonhill *Aberds* 25 H19
Newtonmore *H'land* 24 H15
Newtown Crommelin
Antrim 33 N11
Newtown
Cunningham
Donegal 32 N8
Newtown Forbes
Longford 36 Q8
Newtown Gore
Leitrim 36 P8
Newtown Hamilton
Armagh 33 P10
Newtown *Laois* 40 S9
Newtown *Longford* 36 Q8
Newtown *Tipperary* 39 T7
Newtown
Monasterboice
Louth 37 Q11
Newtown Mount
Kennedy *Wicklow* 37 R11
Newtown St.
Boswells
Scot Borders 21 L18
Newtown Sands
Kerry 38 S5
Newtown *Heref'd* 10 T18
Newtown *Powys* 8 S17
Newtownabbey
Antrim 33 N12
Newtownards *Down* 33 N12
Newtownbreda *Down* 33 N12
Newtownbutler
Fermanagh 32 P9
Newtownshandrum
Cork 39 T6
Newtownstewart
Tyrone 32 N9
Neyland *Pembs* 9 U14
Ninemilehouse
Tipperary 40 T9
Ninfield *E Sussex* 7 W24
Niton *I/Wight* 5 W21
Nobber *Meath* 37 Q10
Nohaval *Cork* 39 U7
Nordelph *Norfolk* 12 S24
Norham *Northum* 21 L19
Normanby le Wold
Lincs 17 R23
Normanton *W Yorks* 16 Q21
North Baddesley
Hants 5 W21
North Berwick *E Loth* 25 K18
North Cerney *Glos* 5 U20
North Charlton
Northum 21 M20
North Elmham
Norfolk 13 S25
North Ferriby
ER Yorks 17 Q22
North Frodingham
ER Yorks 17 Q23
North Hill *Cornw'l* 3 W15
North Hykeham *Lincs* 12 R22
North Kessock
H'land 28 G15
North Molton *Devon* 3 V16
North Newbald
ER Yorks 17 Q22
North Petherton
Som'set 4 V17
North Somercotes
Lincs 17 R24
North Sunderland
Northum 21 L20
North Tawton *Devon* 3 V15
North Thoresby *Lincs* 17 R23
North Tidworth *Wilts* 5 V20
North Walsham
Norfolk 13 S26
North Wingfield
Derby 11 R21
Northallerton *N Yorks* 16 P21
Northam *Devon* 3 V15
Northampton
Northants 11 T22
Northchapel
W Sussex 6 V22
Northfleet *Kent* 7 V24
Northiam *E Sussex* 7 W25
Northleach *Glos* 5 U20
Northop *Flints* 10 R17
Northrepps *Norfolk* 13 S26
Northwich *Ches* 15 R18
Northwold *Norfolk* 12 S24
Northwood *Gtr Lon* 6 U23
Northwood *I/Wight* 5 W21

Norton Fitzwarren
Som'set 4 V17
Norton *Glos* 10 U19
Norton *N Yorks* 17 P22
Norton *Suffolk* 13 T25
Norton *Worcs* 10 T19
Norwich *Norfolk* 13 S26
Nottingham *Nott'ham* 11 S21
Nuneaton *Warwick* 11 S21
Nunney *Som'set* 5 V19
Nurney *Carlow* 40 S10
Nutley *E Sussex* 6 V24
Nutts Corner *Antrim* 33 N11
Nybster *H'land* 29 E17

O

Oadby *Leics* 11 S21
Oakdale *Caerph* 4 U17
Oakengates *Telford* 10 S19
Oakham *Rutl'd* 12 S22
Oban *Arg/Bute* 23 K13
O'briensbridge *Clare* 39 S7
Ochiltree *E Ayrs* 19 M15
Ockley *Surrey* 6 V23
Odiham *Hants* 6 V22
Offord D'Arcy *Cambs* 12 T23
Ogbourne St. George
Wilts 5 V20
Oghill *Londonderry* 32 N9
Oilgate *Wexford* 40 T10
Okehampton *Devon* 3 W15
Old Basing *Hants* 6 V21
Old Bolingbroke
Lincs 12 R24
Old Colwyn *Conwy* 8 R16
Old Deer *Aberds* 29 G19
Old Fletton *Peterbro* 12 S23
Old Leake *Lincs* 12 R24
Old Radnor *Powys* 10 T17
Old Ross *Wexford* 40 T10
Oldbury *S Glos* 4 U18
Oldcastle *Meath* 36 Q9
Oldham *Gtr Man* 15 Q19
Oldleighlin *Carlow* 40 S9
Oldmeldrum *Aberds* 29 H19
Oldtown *Laois* 40 S9
Olgrinmore *H'land* 28 F16
Ollerton *Notts* 11 R21
Olney *M/Keynes* 12 T22
Omagh *Tyrone* 32 N9
Ombersley *Worcs* 10 T19
Omeath *Louth* 37 P11
Onchan *I/Man* 14 P15
Onich *H'land* 23 J13
Oola *Limerick* 39 S7
Oran *Roscommon* 35 Q7
Oranmore *Galway* 35 R6
Ordhead *Aberds* 25 H18
Ordie *Aberds* 25 H18
Orford *Suffolk* 13 T27
Oristown *Meath* 37 Q10
Orleton *Heref'd* 10 T18
Ormesby St.
Margaret *Norfolk* 13 S27
Ormiston *E Loth* 25 L18
Ormskirk *Lancs* 15 Q18
Orpington *Gtr Lon* 6 V24
Orton *Cumb* 15 P18
Osbournby *Lincs* 12 S23
Oskamull *Arg/Bute* 22 K11
Osmotherley *N Yorks* 16 P21
Ossett *W Yorks* 16 Q20
Oswaldtwistle *Lancs* 15 Q19
Oswestry *Shrops* 10 S17
Otford *Kent* 6 V24
Othery *Som'set* 4 V18
Otley *W Yorks* 16 Q20
Otter Ferry *Arg/Bute* 23 K13
Otterburn *Northum* 21 M19
Otterton *Devon* 4 W17
Ottery St. Mary
Devon 4 W17
Oughterard *Galway* 34 R5
Oulton Broad *Suffolk* 13 S27
Oulton *Norfolk* 13 S27
Oundle *Northants* 12 S23
Ousdale *H'land* 28 F16
Outwell *Norfolk* 12 S24
Over *Cambs* 12 T23
Over Wallop *Hants* 5 V20
Overseal *Derby* 11 S20
Overstrand *Norfolk* 13 S26
Overton *Hants* 5 V21
Overton *Wrex* 10 S18

Owston Ferry
N Lincs 17 R22
Oxenholme *Cumb* 15 P18
Oxford *Oxon* 5 U21
Oxnam *Scot Borders* 21 M19
Oxted *Surrey* 6 V24
Oykel Bridge *H'land* 27 G14

P

Pabail *W Isles* 27 F11
Paddock Wood *Kent* 7 V24
Padiham *Lancs* 15 Q19
Padstow *Cornw'l* 2 W14
Paibeil *W Isles* 26 G9
Paignton *Torbay* 3 X16
Pailton *Warwick* 11 T21
Painscastle *Powys* 10 T17
Painshawfield
Northum 21 N20
Painswick *Glos* 5 U19
Paisley *Renf* 19 L15
Palgrave *Suffolk* 13 T26
Pallas Green
Limerick 39 S7
Pallaskenry *Limerick* 39 S6
Palnackie *Dumf/Gal* 19 N16
Pangbourne *W Berks* 5 V21
Papworth Everard
Cambs 12 T23
Park *Galway* 35 R6
Park *Londonderry* 33 N9
Parkeston *Essex* 13 U26
Parkhurst *I/Wight* 5 W21
Parknasilla *Kerry* 38 U4
Parkview *Antrim* 33 N12
Parracombe *Devon* 3 V16
Partney *Lincs* 12 R24
Parton *Cumb* 20 N16
Partry *Mayo* 34 Q5
Passage East
Waterford 40 T10
Passage West *Cork* 39 U7
Pateley Bridge
N Yorks 15 P20
Pathhead *Midloth* 20 L18
Patna *E Ayrs* 19 M15
Patrick Brompton
N Yorks 16 P20
Patrickswell *Limerick* 39 S6
Patrington *ER Yorks* 17 Q23
Patterdale *Cumb* 15 N18
Paull *ER Yorks* 17 Q23
Paulstown *Kilkenny* 40 S9
Paulton
Bath/NE Som'set 4 V18
Peacehaven
E Sussex 6 W23
Peak Forest *Derby* 15 R20
Peasedown St. John
Bath/NE Som'set 5 V19
Peasenhall *Suffolk* 13 T26
Peasmarsh *E Sussex* 7 W25
Peebles
Scot Borders 20 L17
Peel *I/Man* 14 P14
Pegswood *Northum* 21 M20
Pembrey *Carms* 9 U15
Pembridge *Heref'd* 10 T18
Pembroke Dock
Pembs 9 U14
Pembroke *Pembs* 9 U14
Pembury *Kent* 7 V24
Penally *Pembs* 9 U14
Penarth *V/Glam* 4 V17
Pencader *Carms* 9 U15
Pencoed *Bridg* 4 U16
Pendeen *Cornw'l* 2 X12
Penderyn
Rh Cyn Taff 9 U16
Pendine *Carms* 9 U14
Penicuik *Midloth* 20 L17
Penistone *S Yorks* 16 Q20
Penkridge *Staffs* 10 S19
Penmachno *Conwy* 8 R16
Penmaenmawr
Conwy 8 R16
Pennan *Aberds* 29 G19
Pennyghael *Arg/Bute* 22 K11
Penpont *Dumf/Gal* 19 M16
Penrhyndeudraeth
Gwyn 8 S15
Penrith *Cumb* 21 N18
Penryn *Cornw'l* 2 X13
Pensford
Bath/NE Som'set 4 V18

Penshaw *Tyne/Wear* 21 N21
Penshurst *Kent* 6 V24
Pensilva *Cornw'l* 3 X15
Pentraeth *Angl* 8 R15
Pentrefoelas *Conwy* 8 R16
Penworth *Lancs* 15 Q18
Penybont *Powys* 9 T17
Penybontfawr *Powys* 8 S17
Penygroes *Carms* 9 U15
Penygroes *Gwyn* 8 R15
Penysarn *Angl* 8 R15
Penzance *Cornw'l* 2 X12
Perranporth *Cornw'l* 2 X13
Perranzabuloe
Cornw'l 2 X13
Pershore *Worcs* 10 T19
Perth *Perth/Kinr* 24 K17
Peterborough
Peterbro 12 S23
Peterchurch *Heref'd* 10 T18
Peterculter *Aberd C* 25 H19
Peterhead *Aberds* 29 G20
Peterlee *Durham* 21 N21
Petersfield *Hants* 6 V22
Peterswell *Galway* 35 R6
Petham *Kent* 7 V26
Pettigo *Donegal* 32 N8
Petworth *W Sussex* 6 W22
Pevensey *E Sussex* 7 W24
Pewsey *Wilts* 5 V20
Pickering *N Yorks* 17 P22
Piddletrenthide
Dorset 5 W19
Pidley *Cambs* 12 T23
Pilling *Lancs* 15 Q18
Pilton *Som'set* 4 V18
Piltown *Kilkenny* 40 T9
Pinchbeck *Lincs* 12 S23
Pinhoe *Devon* 4 W17
Pinmore Mains
S Ayrs 18 M14
Pinwherry *S Ayrs* 18 M14
Pirbright *Surrey* 6 V22
Pirnmill *N Ayrs* 18 L13
Pitlochry *Perth/Kinr* 24 J16
Pittenweem *Fife* 25 K18
Plean *Stirl* 24 K16
Plockton *H'land* 27 H12
Pluck *Donegal* 32 N8
Pluckley *Kent* 7 V25
Plumbridge *Tyrone* 32 N9
Plumpton *Cumb* 20 N18
Plymouth *Plym'th* 3 X15
Plympton *Plym'th* 3 X15
Plymstock *Plym'th* 3 X15
Pocklington
ER Yorks 17 Q22
Polegate *E Sussex* 7 W24
Polesworth *Warwick* 11 S20
Polloch *H'land* 23 J12
Pollremore *Galway* 35 Q6
Polperro *Cornw'l* 2 X14
Polruan *Cornw'l* 2 X14
Polwarth
Scot Borders 21 L19
Polzeath *Cornw'l* 2 W14
Pomeroy *Tyrone* 33 N10
Pontardawe
Neath P Talb 9 U16
Pontardulais *Swan* 9 U15
Pontefract *W Yorks* 16 Q21
Ponteland *Northum* 21 M20
Ponterwyd *Ceredig'n* 9 T16
Pontesbury *Shrops* 10 S18
Pontoon *Mayo* 35 Q5
Pontrhydfendigaid
Ceredig'n 9 T16
Pontrilas *Heref'd* 10 U18
Pontyates *Carms* 9 U15
Pontyberem *Carms* 9 U15
Pontycymer *Bridg* 9 U16
Pontypool *Torf* 4 U17
Pontypridd
Rh Cyn Taff 9 U17
Pool *Cornw'l* 2 X13
Poole *Poole* 5 W20
Poolewe *H'land* 27 G12
Pooley Bridge *Cumb* 20 N18
Porlock *Som'set* 4 V16
Port Bannatyne
Arg/Bute 18 L13
Port Carlisle *Cumb* 20 N17
Port Charlotte
Arg/Bute 18 L11
Port Ellen *Arg/Bute* 18 L11
Port Erin *I/Man* 14 P14
Port Eynon *Swan* 9 U15
Port Glasgow *Invercl* 19 L14

Port Henderson
  H'land 27 G12
Port Isaac *Cornw'l* 2 W14
Port Logan *Dumf/Gal* 18 N14
Port Nan Giuran
  W Isles 27 F11
Port Nis *W Isles* 27 F11
Port St. Mary *I/Man* 14 P14
Port Talbot
  Neath P Talb 9 U16
Port William
  Dumf/Gal 19 N14
Portacloy *Mayo* 34 P4
Portadown *Armagh* 33 P11
Portaferry *Down* 33 P12
Portarlington *Offaly* 36 R9
Portavadie *Arg/Bute* 18 L13
Portavogie *Down* 33 P13
Portballintrae *Antrim* 33 M10
Portglenone *Antrim* 33 N11
Portgordon *Moray* 29 G17
Porth *Rh Cyn Taff* 9 U17
Porthcawl *Bridg* 4 V16
Porthleven *Cornw'l* 2 X13
Porthmadog *Gwyn* 8 S15
Portishead
  N Som'set 4 V18
Portknockie *Moray* 29 G18
Portlaoise *Laois* 40 R9
Portlaw *Waterford* 40 T9
Portlethen *Aberds* 25 H19
Portmagee *Kerry* 38 U3
Portmahomack
  H'land 28 G16
Portmarnock *Dublin* 37 R11
Portnacroish
  Arg/Bute 23 J13
Portnahaven
  Arg/Bute 18 L10
Porton *Wilts* 5 V20
Portpatrick *Dumf/Gal* 18 N13
Portrane *Dublin* 37 R11
Portreath *Cornw'l* 2 X13
Portree *H'land* 27 H11
Portroe *Tipperary* 39 S7
Portrush *Antrim* 33 M10
Portsalon *Donegal* 32 M8
Portskerra *H'land* 28 E16
Portslade
  Brighton/Hove 6 W23
Portsmouth
  Portsm'th 5 W21
Portsoy *Aberds* 29 G18
Portstewart
  Londonderry 33 M10
Portumna *Galway* 35 R7
Postbridge *Devon* 3 W16
Potter Heigham
  Norfolk 13 S27
Potterne *Wilts* 5 V19
Potters Bar *Herts* 6 U23
Potterspury
  Northants 11 T22
Potton *Beds* 12 T23
Poulton-le-Fylde
  Lancs 15 Q18
Poundstock *Cornw'l* 2 W14
Powick *Worcs* 10 T19
Poynton *Ches* 15 R19
Poyntz Pass *Armagh* 33 P11
Praa Sands *Cornw'l* 2 X13
Prees *Shrops* 10 S18
Preesall *Lancs* 15 Q18
Presbury *Ches* 15 R19
Prescot *Mersey* 15 R18
Prestatyn *Denbs* 8 R17
Prestbury *Glos* 10 U19
Presteigne *Powys* 10 T17
Preston Candover
  Hants 5 V21
Preston *Dorset* 5 W19
Preston *ER Yorks* 17 Q23
Preston *Kent* 7 V26
Preston *Lancs* 15 Q18
Preston *Scot Borders* 21 L19
Prestonpans *E Loth* 25 L18
Prestwich *Gtr Man* 15 R18
Prestwick *S Ayrs* 19 M14
Prestwood *Bucks* 6 U22
Princes Risborough
  Bucks 6 U22
Princetown *Devon* 3 W15
Probus *Cornw'l* 2 X14
Prosperous *Kildare* 37 R10
Prudhoe *Northum* 21 N20
Puckaun *Tipperary* 35 S7
Pucklechurch *S Glos* 5 V19
Puddletown *Dorset* 5 W19
Pudsey *W Yorks* 16 Q20

Pulborough
  W Sussex 6 W22
Pulham Market
  Norfolk 13 T26
Pulham St. Mary
  Norfolk 13 T26
Pumpsaint *Carms* 9 T16
Purfleet *Thurr'k* 7 V24
Purley *Gtr Lon* 6 V23
Purley *W Berks* 6 V21
Purton *Wilts* 5 U20
Puttenham *Surrey* 6 V22
Pwllheli *Gwyn* 8 S15
Pyle *Bridg* 4 U16

Q

Quadring *Lincs* 12 S23
Quainton *Bucks* 6 U22
Quarryfield *Sligo* 35 P6
Quedgeley *Glos* 5 U19
Queenborough *Kent* 7 V25
Queensbury *W Yorks* 15 Q20
Queensferry *Flints* 10 R17
Quilty *Clare* 38 S5
Quin *Clare* 39 S6
Quorndon *Leics* 11 S21

R

Rackenford *Devon* 4 W16
Rackheath *Norfolk* 13 S26
Radcliffe *Gtr Man* 15 Q19
Radcliffe-on-Trent
  Notts 11 S21
Radlett *Herts* 6 U23
Radley *Oxon* 5 U21
Radstock
  Bath/NE Som'set 5 V19
Radyr *Card* 4 U17
Raglan *Monmouths* 4 U18
Rahan *Offaly* 36 R8
Rahara *Roscommon* 36 Q7
Raharney *Westmeath* 36 Q9
Raheen *Tipperary* 39 T8
Rainham *Medway* 7 V25
Rainworth *Notts* 11 R21
Rampark *Louth* 37 P11
Rampside *Cumb* 15 P17
Ramsbottom
  Gtr Man 15 Q19
Ramsbury *Wilts* 5 V20
Ramsey *Cambs* 12 T23
Ramsey *Essex* 13 U26
Ramsey *I/Man* 14 P15
Ramseycleuch
  Scot Borders 20 M17
Ramsgate *Kent* 7 V26
Randalstown *Antrim* 33 N11
Rannoch Station
  Perth/Kinr 24 J14
Raphoe *Donegal* 32 N8
Rasharkin *Antrim* 33 N11
Rath *Offaly* 36 R8
Rathangan *Kildare* 37 R10
Ratharney *Longford* 36 Q8
Rathclogh *Tipperary* 39 S8
Rathconrath
  Westmeath 36 Q8
Rathcool *Cork* 39 T6
Rathcoole *Dublin* 37 R11
Rathcor *Louth* 37 Q11
Rathcormack *Cork* 39 T7
Rathdowney *Laois* 39 S8
Rathdrum *Wicklow* 40 S11
Rathduff *Cork* 39 T6
Rathen *Aberds* 29 G20
Rathfriland *Down* 33 P11
Rathgormuck
  Waterford 39 T9
Rathkeale *Limerick* 39 S6
Rathkenny *Meath* 37 Q10
Rathlacken *Mayo* 34 P5
Rathmelton *Donegal* 32 M8
Rathmolyon *Meath* 37 R10
Rathmore *Kerry* 38 T5
Rathmore *Kildare* 37 R10
Rathmore *Longford* 36 Q8
Rathmullan *Donegal* 32 M8
Rathnew *Wicklow* 40 S11
Rathnure *Wexford* 40 T10
Rathowen
  Westmeath 36 Q8

Rathvilla *Offaly* 36 R9
Rathvilly *Carlow* 40 S10
Ratoath *Meath* 37 Q11
Rattray *Perth/Kinr* 24 J17
Raunds *Northants* 12 T22
Ravenglass *Cumb* 14 P17
Ravensdale *Louth* 37 P11
Ravenshead *Notts* 11 R21
Ravenstonedale
  Cumb 15 P19
Rawcliffe *C/York* 16 Q21
Rawmarsh *S Yorks* 16 R21
Rawtenstall *Lancs* 15 Q19
Rayleigh *Essex* 7 U25
Reading *Reading* 6 V22
Rear Cross *Tipperary* 39 S7
Reay *H'land* 28 E16
Recess *Galway* 34 R4
Red Castle *Donegal* 32 M9
Red Dial *Cumb* 20 N17
Red Point *H'land* 27 G12
Redbourn *Herts* 6 U23
Redbridge *Gtr Lon* 6 U24
Redcar
  Redcar/Clevel'd 16 N21
Redditch *Worcs* 11 T20
Redesmouth
  Northum 21 M19
Redhill *Surrey* 6 V23
Redlynch *Wilts* 5 W20
Redmile *Leics* 11 S22
Redmire *N Yorks* 15 P20
Redruth *Cornw'l* 2 X13
Reedham *Norfolk* 13 S27
Reens *Limerick* 39 S6
Reepham *Norfolk* 13 S26
Reeth *N Yorks* 15 P20
Reiff *H'land* 27 F13
Reigate *Surrey* 6 V23
Reiss *H'land* 29 F17
Renfrew *Renf* 19 L15
Rennington *Northum* 21 M20
Repton *Derby* 11 S20
Resolven
  Neath P Talb 9 U16
Reston *Scot Borders* 21 L19
Retford *Notts* 17 R22
Reydon *Suffolk* 13 T27
Rhayader *Powys* 9 T17
Rhewl *Denbs* 8 R17
Rhiconich *H'land* 27 F14
Rhiw *Gwyn* 8 S14
Rhode *Offaly* 36 R9
Rhondda
  Rh Cyn Taff 9 U17
Rhoose *V/Glam* 4 V17
Rhoslan *Gwyn* 8 S15
Rhosllanerchrugog
  Wrex 10 R17
Rhosneigr *Angl* 8 R14
Rhos-on-Sea *Conwy* 8 R16
Rhossili *Swan* 9 U15
Rhostryfan *Gwyn* 8 R15
Rhubodach *Arg/Bute* 18 L13
Rhuddlan *Denbs* 8 R17
Rhyd-Ddu *Gwyn* 8 R15
Rhyl *Denbs* 8 R17
Rhymney *Caerph* 9 U17
Rhynie *Aberds* 29 H18
Riccall *N Yorks* 16 Q21
Rich Hill *Armagh* 33 P10
Richmond *Gtr Lon* 6 V23
Richmond *N Yorks* 16 P20
Rickmansworth *Herts* 6 U23
Ridsdale *Northum* 21 M19
Rievaulx *N Yorks* 16 P21
Rigside *S Lanarks* 19 L16
Rillington *N Yorks* 17 P22
Ringaskiddy *Cork* 39 U7
Ringford *Dumf/Gal* 19 N15
Ringmer *E Sussex* 6 W24
Ringsend
  Londonderry 33 M10
Ringville *Waterford* 39 T8
Ringwood *Hants* 5 W20
Ripley *Derby* 11 R21
Ripley *N Yorks* 16 P20
Ripley *Surrey* 6 V23
Ripon *N Yorks* 16 P20
Ripponden *W Yorks* 15 Q20
Risca *Caerph* 4 U17
Rishton *Lancs* 15 Q19
Riverchapel *Wexford* 40 S11
Riverstick *Cork* 39 U7
Riverstown *Cork* 39 U7
Riverstown *Sligo* 35 P7
Roade *Northants* 11 T22
Roadhead *Cumb* 20 M18

Roberton
  Scot Borders 20 M18
Robertsbridge
  E Sussex 7 W24
Robertstown *Kildare* 37 R10
Robin Hood's Bay
  N Yorks 17 P22
Rocester *Staffs* 11 S20
Rochdale *Gtr Man* 15 Q19
Roche *Cornw'l* 2 X14
Rochester *Medway* 7 V25
Rochester *Northum* 21 M19
Rochford *Essex* 7 U25
Rochfortbridge
  Westmeath 36 R9
Rockchapel *Cork* 38 T5
Rockcliffe *Cumb* 20 N18
Rockcliffe *Dumf/Gal* 19 N16
Rockcorry *Monaghan* 36 P9
Rockhill *Limerick* 39 T6
Rockingham
  Northants 12 S22
Rockmills *Cork* 39 T7
Rogart *H'land* 28 F15
Rogate *W Sussex* 6 V22
Roghadal *W Isles* 26 G10
Rolvenden *Kent* 7 V25
Romford *Gtr Lon* 6 U24
Romsey *Hants* 5 W21
Roosky *Leitrim* 36 Q8
Ropsley *Lincs* 12 S22
Roscommon
  Roscommon 35 Q7
Roscrea *Tipperary* 36 S8
Rosedale Abbey
  N Yorks 17 P22
Rosegreen *Tipperary* 39 T8
Rosehall *H'land* 28 G14
Rosehearty *Aberds* 29 G19
Rosemarket *Pembs* 9 U14
Rosemarkie *H'land* 28 G15
Rosenallis *Laois* 36 R9
Roskhill *H'land* 26 H10
Roslin *Midloth* 20 L17
Rosmult *Tipperary* 39 S8
Rosneath *Arg/Bute* 23 K14
Ross Carbery *Cork* 38 U5
Ross *Northum* 21 L20
Rossaveel *Galway* 34 R4
Rosscahill *Galway* 35 R5
Rosses Point *Sligo* 32 P6
Rossett *Wrex* 10 R18
Rossinver *Leitrim* 32 P7
Rosslare Harbour
  Wexford 40 T11
Rosslare *Wexford* 40 T11
Rosslea *Fermanagh* 32 P9
Rossnowlagh
  Donegal 32 N7
Ross-on-Wye *Heref'd* 10 U18
Rostellan *Cork* 39 U7
Rostrevor *Down* 37 P11
Rosturk *Mayo* 34 Q4
Rosyth *Fife* 24 K17
Rothbury *Northum* 21 M20
Rotherham *S Yorks* 16 R21
Rothes *Moray* 29 G17
Rothesay *Arg/Bute* 18 L13
Rothienorman
  Aberds 29 H19
Rothwell *Northants* 11 T22
Rothwell *W Yorks* 16 Q21
Rottal *Angus* 25 J17
Rottingdean
  Brighton/Hove 6 W23
Roundstone *Galway* 34 R4
Roundwood *Wicklow* 40 R11
Rousky *Tyrone* 32 N9
Rowanburn *Dumf/Gal* 20 M18
Rowlands Gill
  Tyne/Wear 21 N20
Roxburgh
  Scot Borders 21 L19
Roxby *N Lincs* 17 Q22
Royal Leamington
  Spa *Warwick* 11 T20
Royal Tunbridge
  Wells *Kent* 7 V24
Roybridge *H'land* 23 J14
Royston *Herts* 12 T23
Royston *S Yorks* 16 Q21
Royton *Gtr Man* 15 Q19
Rozel *Chan Is* 2 Z19
Ruabon *Wrex* 10 S17
Ruan *Clare* 35 S6
Ruan Minor *Cornw'l* 2 Y13
Ruardean *Glos* 4 U18
Rubery *Worcs* 10 T19
Rudston *ER Yorks* 17 P23

Rufford *Lancs* 15 Q18
Rugby *Warwick* 11 T21
Rugeley *Staffs* 11 S20
Ruislip *Gtr Lon* 6 U23
Rumburgh *Suffolk* 13 T26
Rumney *Card* 4 U17
Runcorn *Halton* 15 R18
Rush *Dublin* 37 Q11
Rushden *Northants* 12 T22
Rushwick *Worcs* 10 T19
Ruskington *Lincs* 12 R23
Rutherglen *S Lanarks* 19 L15
Ruthin *Denbs* 8 R17
Ruthven *H'land* 24 H15
Ruthwell *Dumf/Gal* 20 N17
Ryal *Northum* 21 M20
Rydal *Cumb* 15 P18
Ryde *I/Wight* 5 W21
Rye *E Sussex* 7 W25
Ryhall *Rutl'd* 12 S23
Ryhope *Tyne/Wear* 21 N21
Ryton *Warwick* 11 T21

S

S. Queensferry
  C/Edinb 24 L17
Sacriston *Durham* 21 N20
Saddell *Arg/Bute* 18 L12
Saffron Walden
  Essex 12 T24
Sageston *Pembs* 9 U14
Saggart *Dublin* 37 R11
St. Abb's
  Scot Borders 25 L19
St. Agnes *Cornw'l* 2 X13
St. Albans *Herts* 6 U23
St. Andrews *Fife* 25 K18
St. Ann's *Dumf/Gal* 20 M17
St. Arvans
  Monmouths 4 U18
St. Asaph *Denbs* 8 R17
St. Athan *V/Glam* 4 V17
St. Aubin *Chan Is* 2 Z19
St. Austell *Cornw'l* 2 X14
St. Bees *Cumb* 14 N16
St. Blazey *Cornw'l* 2 X14
St. Brelade *Chan Is* 2 Z19
St. Breward *Cornw'l* 2 W14
St. Briavels *Glos* 4 U18
St. Bride's Major
  V/Glam 4 V16
St. Buryan *Cornw'l* 2 X12
St. Clears *Carms* 9 U14
St. Columb Major
  Cornw'l 2 X14
St. Columb Minor
  Cornw'l 2 X13
St. Combs *Aberds* 29 G20
St. Cyrus *Aberds* 25 J19
St. David's *Pembs* 9 U13
St. Dennis *Cornw'l* 2 X14
St. Dogmaels
  Ceredig'n 9 T14
St. Dominick *Cornw'l* 3 X15
St. Enoder *Cornw'l* 2 X14
St. Erth *Cornw'l* 2 X13
St. Fergus *Aberds* 29 G20
St. Fillans *Perth/Kinr* 24 K15
St. Germans *Cornw'l* 3 X15
St. Harmon *Powys* 9 T17
St. Helens *Mersey* 15 R18
St. Helier *Chan Is* 2 Z19
St. Issey *Cornw'l* 2 W14
St. Ives *Cambs* 12 T23
St. Ives *Cornw'l* 2 X13
St. Johns Chapel
  Durham 21 N19
St. John's *I/Man* 14 P14
St. Johnstown
  Donegal 32 N9
St. Just *Cornw'l* 2 X12
St. Keverne *Cornw'l* 2 X13
St. Leonards
  E Sussex 5 W25
St. Levan *Cornw'l* 2 X12
St. Mabyn *Cornw'l* 2 W14
St. Margaret's-at-
  Cliffe *Kent* 7 V26
St. Martin *Chan Is* 2 Z18
St. Martin *Chan Is* 2 Z19
St. Mary Bourne
  Hants 5 V21
St. Mary's Bay *Kent* 7 V25
St. Mawes *Cornw'l* 2 X13
St. Mellons *Card* 4 U17

St. Merryn *Cornw'l* 2 W13
St. Minver *Cornw'l* 2 W14
St. Monance *Fife* 25 K18
St. Neots *Cambs* 12 T23
St. Olaves *Norfolk* 13 S27
St. Osyth *Essex* 7 U26
St. Peter Port
  Chan Is 2 Z18
St. Peter *Chan Is* 2 Z19
St. Sampson *Chan Is* 2 Z18
St. Stephen *Cornw'l* 2 X14
St. Teath *Cornw'l* 2 W14
St. Tudy *Cornw'l* 2 W14
Saintfield *Down* 33 P12
Salcombe *Devon* 3 X16
Sale *Gtr Man* 15 R19
Salen *Arg/Bute* 23 J12
Salen *H'land* 23 J12
Salford Priors
  Warwick 11 T20
Salford *Gtr Man* 15 R19
Saline *Fife* 24 K16
Salisbury *Wilts* 5 V20
Sallachy *H'land* 28 F15
Sallahig *Kerry* 38 U3
Sallins *Kildare* 37 R10
Sally Gap *Wicklow* 37 R11
Sallybrook *Cork* 39 U7
Saltash *Cornw'l* 3 X15
Saltburn by the Sea
  Redcar/Clevel'd 17 N22
Saltcoats *N Ayrs* 18 L14
Salterstown *Louth* 37 Q11
Saltfleet *Lincs* 17 R24
Saltfleetby *Lincs* 17 R24
Salthill *Galway* 35 R5
Saltpans *Donegal* 32 M8
Saltwood *Kent* 7 V26
Sampford Courtenay
  Devon 3 W16
Sanaigmore *Arg/Bute* 18 L11
Sandbach *Ches* 10 R19
Sandbank *Arg/Bute* 23 L14
Sandgate *Kent* 7 V26
Sandhead *Dumf/Gal* 18 N14
Sandhurst *Brackn'l* 6 V22
Sandleigh *Oxon* 5 U21
Sandown *I/Wight* 5 W21
Sandringham *Norfolk* 13 S25
Sandwich *Kent* 7 V26
Sandy *Beds* 12 T23
Sanquhar *Dumf/Gal* 19 M16
Sarnau *Ceredig'n* 9 T15
Sarnesfield *Heref'd* 10 T18
Sarre *Kent* 7 V26
Satterthwaite *Cumb* 15 P17
Saundersfoot *Pembs* 9 U14
Sawbridgeworth
  Herts 6 U24
Sawston *Cambs* 12 T24
Sawtry *Cambs* 12 T23
Saxilby *Lincs* 17 R22
Saxlingham
  Nethergate *Norfolk* 13 S26
Saxmundham *Suffolk* 13 T27
Saxthorpe *Norfolk* 13 S26
Scalasaig *Arg/Bute* 22 K11
Scalby *N Yorks* 17 P23
Scamblesby *Lincs* 17 R23
Scarborough *N Yorks* 17 P23
Scardoy *H'land* 27 G14
Scarning *Norfolk* 13 S25
Scarriff *Clare* 39 S6
Scartaglin *Kerry* 38 T5
Scarva *Armagh* 33 P11
Scogh *Kilkenny* 40 T9
Scole *Norfolk* 13 T26
Sconser *H'land* 27 H11
Scopwick *Lincs* 12 R23
Scorton *N Yorks* 16 P20
Scotch Corner
  Monaghan 33 P10
Scotch Corner
  N Yorks 16 P20
Scotstown
  Monaghan 33 P9
Scotter *Lincs* 17 Q22
Scourie *H'land* 27 F13
Scrabster *H'land* 28 E16
Scraghy *Tyrone* 32 N8
Scramoge
  Roscommon 36 Q7
Screeb *Galway* 34 R4
Screggan *Offaly* 36 R8
Scremerston
  Northum 21 L20
Scribbagh
  Fermanagh 32 P7

Scunthorpe *N Lincs* 17 Q22
Sea Palling *Norfolk* 13 S27
Seaford *E Sussex* 6 W24
Seaham *Durham* 21 N21
Seahouses *Northum* 21 L20
Seamer *N Yorks* 17 P23
Seascale *Cumb* 14 P17
Seaton Delaval
  Northum 21 M20
Seaton *Cumb* 20 N16
Seaton *Devon* 4 W17
Seberaham *Cumb* 20 N18
Sedbergh *Cumb* 15 P18
Sedgefield *Durham* 21 N21
Seend *Wilts* 5 V19
Selborne *Hants* 6 V22
Selby *N Yorks* 16 Q21
Selkirk *Scot Borders* 20 L18
Sellafield *Cumb* 14 P17
Selsey *W Sussex* 6 W22
Sennen *Cornw'l* 2 X12
Sennybridge *Powys* 9 U16
Seskinore *Tyrone* 32 N9
Settle *N Yorks* 15 P19
Seven Sisters
  Neath P Talb 9 U16
Sevenoaks *Kent* 6 V24
Severn Beach *S Glos* 4 U18
Severn Stoke *Worcs* 10 T19
Sgarasta Mhor
  W Isles 26 G9
Shaftesbury *Dorset* 5 V19
Shalcombe *I/Wight* 5 W21
Shaldon *Devon* 4 W16
Shalford *Surrey* 6 V22
Shanagolden
  Limerick 38 S5
Shankill *Roscommon* 35 Q7
Shanklin *I/Wight* 5 W21
Shanlaragh *Cork* 38 U5
Shannonbridge *Offaly* 36 R7
Shannow *Cavan* 36 Q9
Shanovogh *Clare* 38 S5
Shantonagh
  Monaghan 37 P10
Shap *Cumb* 15 N18
Sharavogue *Offaly* 36 R8
Sharnbrook *Beds* 12 T22
Sharpness *Glos* 5 U19
Shawbury *Shrops* 10 S18
Shawford *Hants* 5 V21
Shebbear *Devon* 3 W15
Sheerness *Kent* 7 V25
Sheffield *S Yorks* 16 R21
Shefford *Beds* 12 T23
Sheigra *H'land* 27 F13
Shenfield *Essex* 7 U24
Shepherdswell *Kent* 7 V26
Shepley *W Sussex* 16 Q20
Shepshed *Leics* 11 S21
Shepton Mallet
  Som'set 4 V18
Sherborne St. John
  Hants 5 V20
Sherborne *Dorset* 4 W18
Sherburn in Elmet
  N Yorks 16 Q21
Sherburn *N Yorks* 17 P23
Shercock *Cavan* 37 Q10
Shere *Surrey* 6 V23
Sherfield English
  Hants 5 V20
Sherfield on Lodden
  Hants 6 V21
Sheriff Hutton
  N Yorks 16 P21
Sheringham *Norfolk* 13 S26
Sherston *Wilts* 5 U19
Shiel Bridge *H'land* 23 H13
Shieldaig *H'land* 27 G12
Shifnal *Shrops* 10 S19
Shilbottle *Northum* 21 M20
Shildon *Durham* 21 N20
Shillelagh *Wicklow* 40 S10
Shillingstone *Dorset* 5 W19
Shillington *Beds* 12 T23
Shinfield *Wokingham* 6 V22
Shinrone *Offaly* 36 S8
Shipdham *Norfolk* 13 S25
Shipley *W Yorks* 15 Q20
Shipston-on-Stour
  Warwick 11 T20
Shipton under
  Wychwood *Oxon* 5 U20
Shirebrook *Notts* 11 R21
Shoeburyness
  Southend 7 U25
Shoreham by Sea
  W Sussex 6 W23

Shorwell *I/Wight* 5 W21
Shotley Gate *Suffolk* 13 U26
Shottermill *Surrey* 6 V22
Shottisham *Suffolk* 13 T26
Shotts *N Lanarks* 19 L16
Shrewsbury *Shrops* 10 S18
Shrewton *Wilts* 5 V20
Shrigley *Down* 33 P12
Shrivenham *Oxon* 5 U20
Shrule *Mayo* 35 Q5
Siabost *W Isles* 26 F10
Sible Hedingham
  Essex 13 U25
Sibsey *Lincs* 12 R24
Sidbury *Devon* 4 W17
Sidford *Devon* 4 W17
Sidlesham *W Sussex* 6 W22
Sidmouth *Devon* 4 W17
Silloth *Cumb* 20 N17
Silsden *W Yorks* 15 Q20
Silver End *Essex* 7 U25
Silverdale *Lancs* 15 P18
Silvermines *Tipperary* 39 S7
Silverstone *Northants* 11 T21
Silverstream
  Monaghan 33 P10
Silverton *Devon* 4 W17
Simonsbath *Som'set* 4 V16
Single Street
  Donegal 32 P7
Singleton *W Sussex* 6 W22
Sion Mills *Tyrone* 32 N9
Sittingbourne *Kent* 7 V25
Six Crosses *Kerry* 38 T4
Sixmilebridge *Clare* 39 S6
Sixmilecross *Tyrone* 32 N9
Sixpenny Handley
  Dorset 5 W20
Sizewell *Suffolk* 13 T27
Skeagh *Westmeath* 36 Q8
Skegness *Lincs* 12 R24
Skellingthorpe *Lincs* 17 R22
Skelmersdale *Lancs* 15 Q18
Skelmorlie *N Ayrs* 18 L14
Skelton *Cumb* 20 N18
Skelton
  Redcar/Clevel'd 17 N22
Skerries *Dublin* 37 Q11
Skibbereen *Cork* 38 U5
Skinburness *Cumb* 20 N17
Skipness *Arg/Bute* 18 L13
Skipsea *ER Yorks* 17 Q23
Skipton *N Yorks* 15 Q19
Skirlaugh *ER Yorks* 17 Q23
Skull *Cork* 38 U4
Slaidburn *Lancs* 15 Q19
Slaithwaite *W Yorks* 15 Q20
Slaley *Northum* 21 N19
Slamannan *Falk* 19 L16
Slane *Meath* 37 Q10
Sleaford *Lincs* 12 S23
Sledmere *ER Yorks* 17 P22
Sleights *N Yorks* 17 P22
Sligachan *H'land* 27 H11
Sligo *Sligo* 32 P7
Slisgarrow
  Fermanagh 32 P8
Slough *Slough* 6 U22
Smailholm
  Scot Borders 21 L18
Smarden *Kent* 7 V25
Smethwick
  W Midlands 11 S20
Smithborough
  Monaghan 32 P9
Smithfield *Cumb* 20 N18
Snainton *N Yorks* 17 P22
Snaith *ER Yorks* 16 Q21
Snape *Suffolk* 13 T27
Sneaton *N Yorks* 17 P22
Sneem *Kerry* 38 U4
Snettisham *Norfolk* 13 S25
Snodland *Kent* 7 V24
Soham *Cambs* 12 T24
Solas *W Isles* 26 G9
Solihull *W Midlands* 11 T20
Solva *Pembs* 9 U13
Somerby *Leics* 11 S22
Somercotes *Derby* 11 R21
Somersham *Cambs* 12 T23
Somerton *Som'set* 4 V18
Sonning Common
  Oxon 6 U22
Sonning *Wokingham* 6 V22
Sopley *Hants* 5 W20
Sorbie *Dumf/Gal* 19 N15
Sordale *H'land* 28 E17
Sorisdale *Arg/Bute* 22 J11
Sorn *E Ayrs* 19 L15

Sortat *H'land* 29 E17
Soulby *Cumb* 15 P19
South Anston
  S Yorks 16 R21
South Benfleet *Essex* 7 U25
South Brent *Devon* 3 X16
South Cave
  ER Yorks 17 Q22
South Cerney *Glos* 5 U20
South Elkington
  Lincs 17 R23
South Harting
  W Sussex 6 W22
South Hayling *Hants* 6 W22
South Kelsey *Lincs* 17 R23
South Kirkby
  W Yorks 16 Q21
South Molton *Devon* 3 V16
South Ockendon
  Thurr'k 7 U24
South Otterington
  N Yorks 16 P21
South Petherton
  Som'set 4 W18
South Petherwin
  Cornw'l 3 W15
South Shields
  Tyne/Wear 21 N21
South Tawton *Devon* 3 W16
South Tidworth *Wilts* 5 V20
South Walsham
  Norfolk 13 S26
South Warnborough
  Hants 6 V22
South Woodham
  Ferrers *Essex* 7 U25
South Wootton
  Norfolk 12 S24
South Zeal *Devon* 3 W16
Southam *Warwick* 11 T21
Southampton
  S'thampton 5 W20
Southborough *Kent* 7 V24
Southend *Arg/Bute* 18 M12
Southend-on-Sea
  Southend 7 U25
Southery *Norfolk* 12 S24
Southminster *Essex* 7 U25
Southport *Mersey* 15 Q17
Southwark *Gtr Lon* 6 V23
Southwell *Notts* 11 R22
Southwick *W Sussex* 6 W23
Southwold *Suffolk* 13 T27
Sowerby Bridge
  W Yorks 15 Q20
Sowerby *N Yorks* 16 P21
Spa *Kerry* 38 T4
Spalding *Lincs* 12 S23
Spaldwick *Cambs* 12 T23
Spancehill *Clare* 39 S6
Sparkford *Som'set* 4 V18
Spean Bridge *H'land* 23 J14
Speenoge *Donegal* 32 M9
Speke *Mersey* 15 R18
Spennymoor *Durham* 21 N20
Sperrin *Tyrone* 33 N9
Spiddle *Galway* 34 R5
Spilsby *Lincs* 12 R24
Spittal of Glenmuick
  Aberds 25 J17
Spittal *Pembs* 9 U14
Spittle of Glenshee
  Perth/Kinr 24 J17
Spixworth *Norfolk* 13 S26
Spofforth *N Yorks* 16 Q21
Spott *E Loth* 25 L18
Spreyton *Devon* 4 W16
Springfield
  Fermanagh 32 P8
Sproatley *ER Yorks* 17 Q23
Square *Down* 33 P11
Srahmore *Mayo* 34 P4
Srahnalong *Mayo* 34 Q5
Stadhampton *Oxon* 5 U21
Staffin *H'land* 27 G11
Stafford *Staffs* 10 S19
Staindrop *Durham* 21 N20
Staines *Surrey* 6 V22
Stainforth *N Yorks* 15 P19
Stainforth *S Yorks* 16 Q21
Stainton *Lincs* 17 R23
Stainton *Middlesbro* 16 N21
Staintondale *N Yorks* 17 P23
Staithes *N Yorks* 17 N22
Stalbridge *Dorset* 5 W19
Stalham *Norfolk* 13 S27
Stallingborough
  NE Lincs 17 Q23
Stalybridge *Gtr Man* 15 R19

Stamford Bridge
  ER Yorks 17 Q22
Stamford *Lincs* 12 S23
Stamfordham
  Northum 21 M20
Standish *Gtr Man* 15 Q18
Standlake *Oxon* 5 U21
Stanford le Hope
  Thurr'k 7 U24
Stanford on Teme
  Worcs 10 T19
Stanhope *Durham* 21 N19
Stanley *Durham* 21 N20
Stanley *Perth/Kinr* 24 K17
Stannington *Northum* 21 M20
Stansted
  Mountfitchet *Essex* 12 U24
Stanton Harcourt
  Oxon 5 U21
Stanton St. John
  Oxon 5 U21
Stanton *Suffolk* 13 T25
Stanway *Glos* 11 U20
Stanwix *Cumb* 20 N18
Stapleford *Notts* 11 S21
Staplehurst *Kent* 7 V25
Starcross *Devon* 4 W17
Staunton on Wye
  Heref'd 10 T18
Staunton *Glos* 10 U19
Staveley *Cumb* 15 P18
Staveley *Derby* 16 R21
Staxigoe *H'land* 29 F17
Staxton *N Yorks* 17 P23
St.day *Cornw'l* 2 X13
Steeple Bumpstead
  Essex 12 T24
Steeple Claydon
  Bucks 11 U22
Stein *H'land* 26 G10
Stenhousemuir *Falk* 24 K16
Stevenage *Herts* 12 U23
Stevenston *N Ayrs* 19 L14
Stewarton *E Ayrs* 19 L14
Stewartstown *Tyrone* 33 N10
Steyning *W Sussex* 6 W23
Stibb Cross *Devon* 3 W15
Stichill *Scot Borders* 21 L18
Stickford *Lincs* 12 R24
Stickney *Lincs* 12 R24
Stillington *N Yorks* 16 P21
Stillorgan *Dublin* 37 R11
Stilton *Cambs* 12 T23
Stirling *Stirl* 24 K16
Stobbs *Scot Borders* 20 M18
Stobo *Scot Borders* 20 L17
Stock *Essex* 7 U24
Stockbridge *Hants* 5 V21
Stockport *Gtr Man* 15 R19
Stocksbridge
  S Yorks 16 R20
Stockton *Warwick* 11 T21
Stockton-on-Tees
  Stockton 21 N21
Stoer *H'land* 27 F13
Stoke Albany
  Northants 11 T22
Stoke Ferry *Norfolk* 13 S25
Stoke Fleming *Devon* 3 X16
Stoke Gabriel *Devon* 3 X16
Stoke Mandeville
  Bucks 6 U22
Stoke Poges *Bucks* 6 U22
Stoke Prior *Worcs* 10 T19
Stoke *Medway* 7 V25
Stokenchurch *Bucks* 6 U22
Stoke-on-Trent *Stoke* 10 R19
Stokesley *N Yorks* 16 P21
Stone *Bucks* 6 U22
Stone *Glos* 5 U19
Stone *Staffs* 10 S19
Stonehaven *Aberds* 25 J19
Stonehouse *Glos* 5 U19
Stonehouse
  S Lanarks 19 L16
Stoneykirk *Dumf/Gal* 18 N14
Stonham Aspal
  Suffolk 13 T26
Stony Stratford
  M/Keynes 11 T22
Stonyford *Kilkenny* 40 S9
Stornoway *W Isles* 26 F11
Storrington
  W Sussex 6 W23
Stotfold *Beds* 12 T23
Stourbridge
  W Midlands 10 T19
Stourpaine *Dorset* 5 W19
Stourport-on-Severn
  Worcs 10 T19

Stow Bardolph
  Norfolk 12 S24
Stow Scot Borders 20 L18
Stowmarket Suffolk 13 T26
Stow-on-the-Wold
  Glos 11 U20
Strabane Tyrone 32 N9
Strachan Aberds 25 H18
Strachur Arg/Bute 23 K13
Stradbally Kerry 38 T3
Stradbally Laois 40 R9
Stradbally Waterford 40 T9
Stradbroke Suffolk 13 T26
Strade Friary Mayo 35 Q5
Stradone Cavan 36 Q9
Straffan Kildare 37 R10
Straiton S Ayrs 19 M14
Strandhill Sligo 32 P6
Strangford Down 33 P12
Stranorlar Donegal 32 N8
Stranraer Dumf/Gal 18 N13
Stratford St. Mary
  Suffolk 13 U25
Stratford-Upon-Avon
  Warwick 11 T20
Strathan H'land 28 E15
Strathaven S Lanarks 19 L15
Strathblane Stirl 24 L15
Strathdon Aberds 25 H17
Strathkanaird H'land 27 G13
Strathpeffer H'land 28 G14
Strathy H'land 28 E16
Strathyre Stirl 24 K15
Stratmiglo Fife 24 K17
Stratton St. Margaret
  Swindon 5 U20
Stratton Cornw'l 2 W14
Stratton Glos 5 U20
Streamstown Galway 34 Q3
Streatley W Berks 5 U21
Street Som'set 4 V18
Strensall C/York 16 P21
Stretford Gtr Man 15 R19
Stretham Cambs 12 S22
Stretton Rutl'd 12 S22
Stretton Staffs 11 S20
Stretton Warrington 15 R18
Strichen Aberds 29 G19
Strokestown
  Roscommon 36 Q7
Stromeferry H'land 27 H12
Stromemore H'land 27 H12
Stronachlachar Stirl 24 K14
Strone Arg/Bute 23 L14
Strontian H'land 23 J12
Stroove Donegal 33 M10
Stroud Glos 5 U19
Struy H'land 28 H14
Stubbington Hants 5 W21
Studland Dorset 5 W20
Studley Warwick 11 T20
Sturminster Marshall
  Dorset 5 W19
Sturminster Newton
  Dorset 5 W19
Sturry Kent 7 V26
Sturton Lincs 17 R22
Sudbury Derby 11 S20
Sudbury Suffolk 13 T25
Sulby I/Man 14 P15
Sully V/Glam 4 V17
Summerhill Meath 37 R10
Sunderland
  Tyne/Wear 21 N21
Sunk Island
  ER Yorks 17 Q23
Sunninghill Windsor 6 V22
Sutterton Lincs 12 S23
Sutton Bridge Lincs 12 S24
Sutton Coldfield
  W Midlands 11 S20
Sutton Courtenay
  Oxon 5 U21
Sutton Lane Ends
  Ches 15 R19
Sutton Scotney
  Hants 5 V21
Sutton Cambs 12 T24
Sutton Gtr Lon 6 V23
Sutton Valence Kent 7 V25
Sutton-in-Ashfield
  Notts 11 R21
Sutton-on-Sea Lincs 17 R24
Sutton-on-Trent
  Notts 11 R22
Sutton-under-
  Whitestonecliffe
  N Yorks 16 P21
Swadlincote Derby 11 S20

Swaffham Norfolk 13 S25
Swalcliffe Oxon 11 T21
Swalecliffe Kent 7 V26
Swan Laois 40 S9
Swanage Dorset 5 W20
Swanley Kent 6 V24
Swanlinbar Cavan 32 P8
Swansea Swan 9 U16
Swatragh
  Londonderry 33 N10
Sway Hants 5 W20
Swindon Swindon 5 U20
Swinefleet ER Yorks 17 Q22
Swineshead Lincs 12 S23
Swinford Mayo 35 Q6
Swinton Gtr Man 15 Q19
Swinton S Yorks 16 R21
Swinton
  Scot Borders 21 L19
Swords Dublin 37 R11
Symington S Lanarks 20 L16
Symonds Yat Heref'd 4 U18
Syresham Northants 11 T21
Syston Leics 11 S21

T

Tadcaster N Yorks 16 Q21
Tadley Hants 5 V21
Taghmon Wexford 40 T10
Tain H'land 28 G15
Talgarth Powys 10 U17
Talladale H'land 27 G12
Tallaght Dublin 37 R11
Tallanstown Louth 37 Q10
Talley Carms 9 U15
Tallow Waterford 39 T7
Tallowbridge
  Waterford 39 T7
Talsarnau Gwyn 8 S15
Talybont Ceredig'n 8 T16
Tal-y-llyn Gwyn 8 S16
Talysarn Gwyn 8 R15
Tamerton Foliot
  Plym'th 3 X15
Tamworth Staffs 11 S20
Tandragee Armagh 33 P11
Tang Longford 36 Q8
Tangmere W Sussex 6 W22
Tannadice Angus 25 J18
Tanworth Warwick 11 T20
Taobh Tuath W Isles 26 G9
Tara Meath 37 Q10
Tarbert Kerry 38 S5
Tarbert Arg/Bute 18 L13
Tarbet Arg/Bute 24 K14
Tarbet H'land 23 J12
Tarbolton S Ayrs 19 L15
Tarland Aberds 25 H18
Tarleton Lancs 15 Q18
Tarporley Ches 10 R18
Tarrant Hinton Dorset 5 W19
Tarskavaig H'land 23 H12
Tarves Aberds 29 H19
Tarvin Ches 10 R18
Tattenhall Ches 10 R18
Tattersett Norfolk 13 S25
Taunton Som'set 4 V17
Taur Cork 38 T5
Tavistock Devon 3 W15
Tawnyinah Mayo 35 Q6
Tayinloan Arg/Bute 18 L12
Taynuilt Arg/Bute 23 K13
Tayport Fife 25 K18
Teangue H'land 23 H12
Tebay Cumb 15 P18
Tedavnet Monaghan 32 P8
Tedburn St Mary
  Devon 4 W16
Teeshan Antrim 33 N11
Teignmouth Devon 4 W16
Telford Telford 10 S19
Temple Combe
  Som'set 5 W19
Temple Ewell Kent 7 V26
Temple Sowerby
  Cumb 21 N18
Templeboy Sligo 35 P6
Templederry
  Tipperary 39 S7
Templemore
  Tipperary 39 S8
Templenoe Kerry 38 U5
Templepatrick Antrim 33 N11
Templeton Pembs 9 U14
Templetouhy
  Tipperary 39 S8

Tempo Fermanagh 32 P9
Tenbury Wells
  Heref'd 10 T18
Tenby Pembs 9 U14
Tenterden Kent 7 V25
Termon Cavan 32 P8
Termon Donegal 32 M8
Termonfeckin Louth 37 Q11
Terrington St.
  Clement Norfolk 12 S24
Terrington N Yorks 17 P22
Terryglass Tipperary 36 R7
Tetbury Glos 5 U19
Tetney Lincs 17 R23
Tetsworth Oxon 6 U22
Teviothead
  Scot Borders 20 M18
Tewkesbury Glos 10 U19
Teynham Kent 7 V25
Thame Oxon 6 U22
Thatcham W Berks 5 V21
Thaxted Essex 12 U24
The Downs
  Westmeath 36 Q9
The Loup
  Londonderry 33 N10
The Mumbles Swan 9 U16
The Sheddings
  Antrim 33 N11
The Temple Down 33 P12
Theale W Berks 6 V21
Thetford Norfolk 13 T25
Thirsk N Yorks 16 P21
Thomas Street
  Roscommon 35 R7
Thomastown
  Kilkenny 40 S9
Thornaby on Tees
  Stockton 21 N21
Thornbury S Glos 4 U18
Thorndon Suffolk 13 T26
Thorne S Yorks 17 Q22
Thorney Peterbro 12 S23
Thornham Norfolk 13 S25
Thornhill Dumf/Gal 19 M16
Thornhill Stirl 24 K15
Thornthwaite Cumb 20 N17
Thornton Dale
  N Yorks 17 P22
Thornton Lancs 15 Q17
Thorpe le Soken
  Essex 7 U26
Thorpe Norfolk 13 S26
Thorverton Devon 4 W16
Thrapston Northants 12 T22
Three Legged Cross
  Dorset 5 W20
Threlkeld Cumb 20 N17
Threshfield N Yorks 15 P19
Thrumster H'land 29 F17
Thurcroft S Yorks 16 R21
Thurlby Lincs 12 S23
Thurles Tipperary 39 S8
Thurlestone Devon 3 X16
Thurmaston Leics 11 S21
Thursby Cumb 20 N17
Thurso H'land 28 E16
Ticehurst E Sussex 7 V24
Tickhill S Yorks 16 R21
Tideswell Derby 15 R20
Tighnabruaich
  Arg/Bute 18 L13
Tilbury Thurr'k 7 V24
Tillicoultry Clack 24 K16
Tillingham Essex 7 U25
Tilmanstone Kent 7 V26
Timahoe Kildare 37 R10
Timahoe Laois 40 S9
Timberscombe
  Som'set 4 V16
Timoleague Cork 39 U6
Timolin Kildare 40 S10
Timsbury
  Bath/NE Som'set 5 V19
Tinahely Wicklow 40 S11
Tingewick Bucks 11 U21
Tintagel Cornw'l 2 W14
Tintern Abbey
  Wexford 40 T10
Tintern Monmouths 4 U18
Tipperary Tipperary 39 T7
Tipton W Midlands 10 S19
Tiptree Essex 7 U25
Tisbury Wilts 5 V19
Titchfield Hants 5 W21
Tiverton Devon 4 W17
Tobercurry Sligo 35 P6
Tobermoney Down 33 P12
Tobermore
  Londonderry 33 N10

Tobermory Arg/Bute 22 J11
Toberonochy
  Arg/Bute 23 K12
Toberoe Galway 35 R6
Tobha Mor W Isles 26 H9
Toddington Beds 12 U22
Todmorden W Yorks 15 Q19
Togher Cork 38 U5
Togher Louth 37 Q11
Tolastadh bho
  Thuath W Isles 27 F11
Tollesbury Essex 7 U25
Tolpuddle Dorset 5 W19
Tomatin H'land 28 H16
Tomdoun H'land 23 H13
Tomintoul Moray 24 H17
Tomnavoulin Moray 28 H17
Tonbridge Kent 7 V24
Tondu Bridg 4 U16
Tong Shrops 10 S19
Tongue H'land 28 F15
Tonyrefail
  Rh Cyn Taff 9 U17
Toomakeady Mayo 34 Q5
Toombeola Galway 34 R4
Toome Antrim 33 N11
Toomyvara Tipperary 39 S7
Toormore Cork 38 U4
Topcliffe N Yorks 16 P21
Topsham Devon 4 W17
Torcross Devon 3 X16
Torness H'land 28 H15
Torphins Aberds 25 H18
Torpoint Cornw'l 3 X15
Torquay Torbay 3 X16
Torridon H'land 27 G12
Torroble H'land 28 F15
Torteval Chan Is 2 Z18
Torthorwald
  Dumf/Gal 20 M16
Torver Cumb 15 P17
Toscaig H'land 27 H12
Totland I/Wight 5 W20
Totley S Yorks 16 R20
Totnes Devon 3 X16
Totton Hants 5 W20
Tow Law Durham 21 N20
Towcester Northants 11 T22
Tower Hamlets
  Gtr Lon 6 U23
Town Yetholm
  Scot Borders 21 L19
Trafford Park
  Gtr Man 15 R19
Tralee Kerry 38 T4
Tramore Waterford 40 T9
Tranent E Loth 25 L18
Trawsfynydd Gwyn 8 S16
Trecastle Powys 9 U16
Tredegar Bl Gwent 4 U17
Trefeglwys Powys 8 S16
Trefnant Denbs 8 R17
Trefriw Conwy 8 R16
Tregaron Ceredig'n 9 T16
Tregony Cornw'l 2 X14
Tregynon Powys 8 S17
Treharris Merth Tyd 9 U17
Trelech Carms 9 U15
Tremadog Gwyn 8 S15
Trenance Cornw'l 2 X13
Trentham Stoke 10 S19
Treorchy Rh Cyn Taff 9 U17
Tresilian Cornw'l 2 X13
Tretower Powys 10 U17
Treuddyn Flints 10 R17
Trillick Tyrone 32 P9
Trim Meath 37 Q10
Trimdon Durham 21 N21
Trimley Suffolk 13 U26
Tring Herts 6 U22
Trinity Chan Is 2 Z19
Troon S Ayrs 19 L14
Troutbeck Cumb 15 P18
Trowbridge Wilts 5 V19
Trull Som'set 4 W17
Trumpington Cambs 12 T24
Trunch Norfolk 13 S26
Truro Cornw'l 2 X13
Tuam Galway 35 Q6
Tuamgraney Clare 39 S6
Tubber Galway 35 R6
Tuddenham Suffolk 13 T25
Tudweiliog Gwyn 8 S14
Tulla Clare 39 S6
Tullaghan Leitrim 32 P7
Tullaghoge Tyrone 33 N10
Tullaghought
  Kilkenny 40 T9
Tullagower Clare 38 S5

Tullamore Offaly 36 R9
Tullaroan Kilkenny 40 S9
Tullow Carlow 40 S10
Tully Cross Galway 34 Q4
Tully Roscommon 36 Q7
Tullybeg Galway 35 Q6
Tullycrossmearan
  Fermanagh 32 P8
Tullymacreeve
  Armagh 37 P11
Tullynessle Aberds 29 H18
Tullyverry
  Londonderry 32 M9
Tullyvin Cavan 36 P9
Tulsk Roscommon 35 Q7
Tummel Bridge
  Perth/Kinr 24 J15
Tummery Tyrone 32 P8
Tunstall Suffolk 13 T26
Turloughmore
  Galway 35 R6
Turnberry S Ayrs 18 M14
Turreen Longford 36 Q8
Turriff Aberds 29 G19
Turvey Beds 12 T22
Tutbury Staffs 11 S20
Tuxford Notts 17 R22
Tweedmouth
  Northum 21 L18
Tweedshaws
  Scot Borders 20 M16
Tweedsmuir
  Scot Borders 20 L17
Twenty Lincs 12 S23
Twomileborris
  Tipperary 39 S8
Twyford Hants 5 V21
Twyford Leics 11 S22
Twyford Wokingham 6 V22
Tydd St. Giles
  Cambs 12 S24
Tydd St. Mary Lincs 12 S24
Tylorstown
  Rh Cyn Taff 9 U17
Tynagh Galway 35 R7
Tynan Armagh 33 P10
Tyndrum Stirl 24 K14
Tynemouth
  Tyne/Wear 21 M21
Ty'n-y-groes Conwy 8 R16
Tyrrellspass
  Westmeath 36 R9
Tywardreath Cornw'l 2 X14
Tywyn Gwyn 8 S15

U

Uckfield E Sussex 6 W24
Uddingston
  S Lanarks 19 L15
Uffculme Devon 4 W17
Uffington Oxon 5 U20
Ufford Suffolk 13 T26
Ugborough Devon 3 X16
Uig H'land 26 G11
Ulbster H'land 29 F17
Ulceby Cross Lincs 17 R24
Ulceby N Lincs 17 Q23
Uley Glos 5 U19
Ullapool H'land 27 G13
Ulverston Cumb 15 P17
Unapool H'land 27 F13
Upavon Wilts 5 V20
Uphill N Som'set 4 V18
Upper Chapel Powys 9 T17
Upper Heyford Oxon 11 U21
Upper Hindhope
  Scot Borders 21 M19
Upper Poppleton
  C/York 16 Q21
Upper Tean Staffs 11 S20
Upperchurch
  Tipperary 39 S7
Uppingham Rutl'd 12 S22
Upton Snodsbury
  Worcs 10 T19
Upton Ches 15 R18
Upton-upon-Severn
  Worcs 10 T19
Upwey Dorset 5 W19
Urchfont Wilts 5 V20
Urlingford Kilkenny 39 S8
Urmston Gtr Man 15 R19
Usk Monmouths 4 U18
Usselby Lincs 17 R23
Uttoxeter Staffs 11 S20

V

Valley *Angl*	8	R14
Ventnor *I/Wight*	5	W21
Ventry *Kerry*	38	T3
Verwood *Dorset*	5	W20
Veryan *Cornw'l*	2	X14
Vicarstown *Laois*	40	R9
Vickerstown *Cumb*	14	P17
Virginia *Cavan*	36	Q9
Virginia Water *Surrey*	6	V22

W

Waddesdon *Bucks*	6	U22
Waddingham *Lincs*	17	R22
Waddington *Wexford*	40	T10
Waddington *Lincs*	12	R22
Wadebridge *Cornw'l*	2	W14
Wadhurst *E Sussex*	7	V24
Wainfleet All Saints *Lincs*	13	R22
Wakefield *W Yorks*	16	Q21
Walberswick *Suffolk*	13	T27
Walcott *Lincs*	12	R23
Walderslade *Medway*	7	V25
Waldron *E Sussex*	6	W24
Walford *Heref'd*	10	T18
Walkerburn *Scot Borders*	20	L18
Walkeringham *Notts*	17	R22
Wallasey *Mersey*	15	R17
Wallingford *Oxon*	5	U21
Wallsend *Tyne/Wear*	21	N20
Walmer *Kent*	7	V26
Walpole *Norfolk*	12	S23
Walsall *W Midlands*	11	S20
Walsham le Willows *Suffolk*	13	T25
Walsoken *Cambs*	12	S24
Waltham Abbey *Essex*	6	U24
Waltham Forest *Gtr Lon*	6	U24
Waltham on the Wolds *Leics*	11	S22
Waltham *NE Lincs*	17	Q23
Walton *Cumb*	21	N18
Walton-on-Thames *Surrey*	6	V23
Walton-on-the-Naze *Essex*	7	U26
Wanborough *Swindon*	5	U20
Wandsworth *Gtr Lon*	6	V23
Wangford *Suffolk*	13	T27
Wansford *Peterbro*	12	S23
Wantage *Oxon*	5	U21
Warboys *Cambs*	12	T23
Ward *Dublin*	37	R11
Wardington *Oxon*	11	T21
Wardle *Ches*	10	R18
Ware *Herts*	6	U23
Wareham *Dorset*	5	W19
Wargrave *Wokingham*	6	V22
Waringstown *Down*	33	P11
Wark *Northum*	21	M19
Warkworth *Northum*	21	M20
Warley *W Midlands*	11	T20
Warminster *Wilts*	5	V19
Warrenpoint *Down*	37	P11
Warrington *Warrington*	15	R18
Warton *Lancs*	15	P18
Warwick *Warwick*	11	T20
Washaway *Cornw'l*	2	X14
Washford *Som'set*	4	V17
Washingborough *Lincs*	17	R23
Washington *Tyne/Wear*	21	N20
Washington *W Sussex*	6	W23
Watchet *Som'set*	4	V17
Watchfield *Oxon*	5	U20
Waterbeach *Cambs*	12	T24
Waterford *Waterford*	40	T9
Watergrasshill *Cork*	39	T7
Waterhead *Angus*	25	J18
Waterhouses *Staffs*	11	R20
Wateringbury *Kent*	7	V24
Waterlooville *Hants*	6	W21
Waterside *Londonderry*	32	N9

Waterville *Kerry*	38	U3
Watford *Herts*	6	U23
Wath upon Dearne *S Yorks*	16	R21
Watlington *Norfolk*	12	S24
Watlington *Oxon*	6	U22
Watten *H'land*	28	F17
Watton *Norfolk*	13	S25
Waunfawr *Gwyn*	8	R15
Weachyburn *Aberds*	29	G18
Wearhead *Durham*	21	N19
Weasenham *Norfolk*	13	S25
Weaverham *Ches*	15	R18
Weaverthorpe *N Yorks*	17	P22
Wedmore *Som'set*	4	V18
Wednesbury *W Midlands*	10	S19
Wednesfield *W Midlands*	10	S19
Weedon Bec *Northants*	11	T21
Weeley *Essex*	7	U26
Welborn *Lincs*	12	R22
Weldon *Northants*	12	T22
Weldon *Northum*	21	M20
Welford *Northants*	11	T21
Welford *W Berks*	5	V21
Wellesbourne *Warwick*	11	T20
Wellingborough *Northants*	12	T22
Wellington *Som'set*	4	W17
Wellington *Telford*	10	S18
Wellingtonbridge *Wexford*	40	T10
Wellow *Bath/NE Som'set*	5	V19
Wells *Som'set*	4	V18
Wells-next-the-Sea *Norfolk*	13	S25
Welney *Norfolk*	12	S24
Welshampton *Shrops*	10	S18
Welshpool *Powys*	10	S17
Welton *Lincs*	17	R23
Welwyn Garden City *Herts*	6	U23
Wem *Shrops*	10	S18
Wembury *Devon*	3	X15
Wemyss Bay *Invercl*	18	L14
Wendover *Bucks*	6	U22
Wensley *N Yorks*	15	P20
Wenvoe *V/Glam*	4	V17
Weobley *Heref'd*	10	T18
Werrington *Cornw'l*	3	W15
West Auckland *Durham*	21	N20
West Bergholt *Essex*	13	U25
West Bridgford *Notts*	11	S21
West Bromwich *W Midlands*	11	S20
West Burton *N Yorks*	15	P20
West Calder *W Loth*	20	L16
West Coker *Som'set*	4	W18
West Dean *Wilts*	5	V20
West End *Hants*	5	W21
West Felton *Shrops*	10	S18
West Grinstead *W Sussex*	6	W23
West Haddon *Northants*	11	T21
West Kilbride *N Ayrs*	18	L14
West Kingsdown *Kent*	7	V24
West Kirby *Mersey*	15	R17
West Linton *Scot Borders*	20	L17
West Looe *Cornw'l*	3	X15
West Lulworth *Dorset*	5	W19
West Malling *Kent*	7	V24
West Meon *Hants*	5	V21
West Mersea *Essex*	7	U25
West Moors *Dorset*	5	W20
West Rasen *Lincs*	17	R23
West Thorney *W Sussex*	6	W22
West Wellow *Hants*	5	W20
West Woodburn *Northum*	21	M19
Westbourne *W Sussex*	6	W22
Westbury *Shrops*	10	S18
Westbury *Wilts*	5	V19
Westbury-on-Severn *Glos*	5	U19
Westbury-sub-Mendip *Som'set*	4	V18
Westcott *Surrey*	6	V23

Westerham *Kent*	6	V24
Westfield *E Sussex*	7	W25
Westhill *Aberds*	25	H19
Westhoughton *Gtr Man*	15	Q18
Westleton *Suffolk*	13	T27
Westminster *Gtr Lon*	6	U23
Weston *Staffs*	10	S19
Weston-Super-Mare *N Som'set*	4	V18
Westonzoyland *Som'set*	4	V18
Westport *Mayo*	34	Q4
Westruther *Scot Borders*	21	L18
Westward Ho! *Devon*	3	V15
Wetheral *Cumb*	20	N18
Wetherby *W Yorks*	16	Q21
Wetwang *ER Yorks*	17	P22
Wexford *Wexford*	40	T11
Weybourne *Norfolk*	13	S26
Weybridge *Surrey*	6	V23
Weyhill *Hants*	5	V20
Weymouth *Dorset*	5	W19
Whaley Bridge *Derby*	15	R20
Whalley *Lancs*	15	Q19
Whalton *Northum*	21	M20
Whaplode *Lincs*	12	S23
Whatton *Notts*	11	S22
Whauphill *Dumf/Gal*	19	N14
Wheathampstead *Herts*	6	U23
Wheathill *Fermanagh*	32	P8
Wheatley Hill *Durham*	21	N21
Wheatley *Notts*	17	R22
Wheatley *Oxon*	5	U21
Wheaton Aston *Staffs*	10	S19
Wheldrake *C/York*	17	Q22
Whicham *Cumb*	14	P17
Whickham *Tyne/Wear*	21	N20
Whimple *Devon*	4	W17
Whipsnade *Beds*	6	U22
Whissendine *Rutl'd*	11	S22
Whitburn *W Loth*	20	L16
Whitby *N Yorks*	17	P22
Whitchurch *Bristol*	4	V18
Whitchurch *Bucks*	6	U22
Whitchurch *Devon*	3	W15
Whitchurch *Hants*	5	V21
Whitchurch *Heref'd*	4	U18
Whitchurch *Shrops*	10	S18
White Bridge *H'land*	24	H14
White Castle *Donegal*	32	M9
Whitecross *Armagh*	33	P11
Whitegate *Clare*	35	S7
Whitegate *Cork*	39	U7
Whitehaven *Cumb*	20	N16
Whitehead *Antrim*	33	N12
Whitehill *Fermanagh*	32	P8
Whitehouse *Arg/Bute*	18	L13
Whitekirk *E Loth*	25	K18
Whiteparish *Wilts*	5	V20
Whitfield *Kent*	7	V26
Whithorn *Dumf/Gal*	19	N15
Whitland *Carms*	9	U14
Whitley Bay *Tyne/Wear*	21	M21
Whitsome *Scot Borders*	21	L19
Whitstable *Kent*	7	V26
Whitstone *Cornw'l*	3	W15
Whittington *Derby*	16	R21
Whittington *Lancs*	15	P18
Whittington *Shrops*	10	S18
Whittington *Staffs*	11	S20
Whittlebury *Northants*	11	T22
Whittlesey *Cambs*	12	S23
Whittlesford *Cambs*	12	T24
Whitwell *Derby*	16	R21
Whitwell *I/Wight*	5	W21
Whitwick *Leics*	11	S21
Whitworth *Lancs*	15	Q19
Whixley *N Yorks*	16	P21
Wick *H'land*	29	F17
Wick *S Glos*	5	V19
Wick *V/Glam*	4	V16
Wick *Wilts*	5	W20
Wicken *Cambs*	12	T24
Wickford *Essex*	7	U25
Wickham Market *Suffolk*	13	T26
Wickham *Hants*	5	W21
Wicklow *Wicklow*	40	S11
Wickwar *S Glos*	5	U19
Widdrington *Northum*	21	M20

Wide Open *Tyne/Wear*	21	M20
Widecombe *Devon*	3	W16
Widemouth *Cornw'l*	2	W14
Widnes *Halton*	15	R18
Wigan *Gtr Man*	15	Q18
Wigmore *Heref'd*	10	T18
Wigmore *Medway*	7	V25
Wigston *Leics*	11	S21
Wigton *Cumb*	20	N17
Wigtown *Dumf/Gal*	19	N15
Willand *Devon*	4	W17
Willaston *Ches*	15	R17
Willenhall *W Midlands*	10	S19
Willersley *Heref'd*	10	T17
Willesborough *Kent*	7	V25
Williamstown *Galway*	35	Q6
Willingdon *E Sussex*	7	W24
Willington *Beds*	12	T23
Willington *Durham*	21	N20
Williton *Som'set*	4	V17
Willoughby *Lincs*	17	R24
Wilmington *Devon*	4	W17
Wilmslow *Ches*	15	R19
Wilnecote *Staffs*	11	S20
Wilton *Wilts*	5	V20
Wimblington *Cambs*	12	S24
Wimborne Minster *Dorset*	5	W20
Wincanton *Som'set*	5	V19
Winchcombe *Glos*	11	U20
Winchelsea *E Sussex*	7	W25
Winchester *Hants*	5	V21
Windermere *Cumb*	15	P18
Windgap *Kilkenny*	40	T9
Windsor *Windsor*	6	V22
Windygates *Fife*	25	K17
Wing *Bucks*	6	U22
Wingate *Durham*	21	N21
Wingham *Kent*	7	V26
Winkleigh *Devon*	3	W16
Winscombe *N Som'set*	4	V18
Winsford *Ches*	10	R18
Winslow *Bucks*	11	U22
Winster *Derby*	11	R20
Winston *Durham*	21	N20
Winterborne Abbas *Dorset*	4	W18
Winterborne Stickland *Dorset*	5	W19
Winterton *N Lincs*	17	Q22
Winterton *Norfolk*	13	S27
Wirksworth *Derby*	11	R20
Wisbech St. Mary *Cambs*	12	S24
Wisbech *Cambs*	12	S24
Wisborough Green *W Sussex*	6	V23
Wishaw *N Lanarks*	19	L16
Witchampton *Dorset*	5	W19
Witchford *Cambs*	12	T24
Witham *Essex*	7	U25
Witheridge *Devon*	4	W16
Withern *Lincs*	17	R24
Withernsea *ER Yorks*	17	Q24
Withington *Glos*	5	U20
Witley *Surrey*	6	V22
Witnesham *Suffolk*	13	T26
Witney *Oxon*	5	U21
Wittersham *Kent*	7	V25
Wiveliscombe *Som'set*	4	V17
Wivelsfield *E Sussex*	6	W23
Wivenhoe *Essex*	7	U25
Wix *Essex*	13	U26
Woburn Sands *M/Keynes*	12	T22
Woburn *Beds*	12	U22
Woking *Surrey*	6	V22
Wokingham *Wokingham*	6	V22
Wolf's Castle *Pembs*	9	U14
Wollaston *Northants*	12	T22
Wolsingham *Durham*	21	N20
Wolverhampton *W Midlands*	10	S19
Wolverton *M/Keynes*	11	T22
Wolviston *Stockton*	21	N21
Wombwell *S Yorks*	16	Q21
Wonersh *Surrey*	6	V22
Wonston *Hants*	5	V21
Woodbridge *Suffolk*	13	T26
Woodbury *Devon*	4	W17
Woodchester *Glos*	5	U19
Woodchurch *Kent*	7	V25
Woodcote *Oxon*	6	U21

Woodenbridge *Wicklow*	40	S11
Woodford *Galway*	35	R7
Woodgreen *Hants*	5	W20
Woodhall Spa *Lincs*	12	R23
Woodhouse Eaves *Leics*	11	S21
Woodhouse *S Yorks*	16	R21
Woodlawn *Galway*	35	R7
Woodley *Wokingham*	6	V22
Woodstock *Oxon*	5	U21
Woodtown *Meath*	37	Q10
Woofferton *Shrops*	10	T18
Wookey Hole *Som'set*	4	V18
Wookey *Som'set*	4	V18
Wool *Dorset*	5	W19
Woolacombe *Devon*	3	V15
Woolavington *Som'set*	4	V18
Wooler *Northum*	21	L19
Woolwich *Gtr Lon*	6	V24
Wooperton *Northum*	21	M20
Woore *Shrops*	10	S19
Wootton Bassett *Wilts*	5	U20
Wootton Bridge *I/Wight*	5	W21
Wootton Wawen *Warwick*	11	T20
Worcester *Worcs*	10	T19
Worfield *Shrops*	10	S19
Workington *Cumb*	20	N16
Worksop *Notts*	16	R21
Wormit *Fife*	25	K18
Worsbrough *S Yorks*	16	Q21
Wortham *Suffolk*	13	T26
Worthing *W Sussex*	6	W23
Wotton under Edge *Glos*	5	U19
Wragby *Lincs*	17	R23
Wrangle *Lincs*	12	R24
Wrea Green *Lancs*	15	Q18
Wrentham *Suffolk*	13	T27
Wretham *Norfolk*	13	T25
Wrexham *Wrex*	10	R17
Writtle *Essex*	7	U24
Wroughton *Swindon*	5	U20
Wroxham *Norfolk*	13	S26
Wroxton *Oxon*	11	T21
Wyberton *Lincs*	12	S23
Wye *Kent*	7	V25
Wylye *Wilts*	5	V20
Wymondham *Leics*	12	S22
Wymondham *Norfolk*	13	S26

Y

Y Felinheli *Gwyn*	8	R15
Yalding *Kent*	7	V24
Yarcombe *Devon*	4	W17
Yardley Hastings *Northants*	12	T22
Yarm *Stockton*	16	N21
Yarmouth *I/Wight*	5	W21
Yarnton *Oxon*	5	U21
Yarrow *Scot Borders*	20	L17
Yate *S Glos*	5	U19
Yatton *N Som'set*	4	V18
Yaxley *Cambs*	12	S23
Yeadon *W Yorks*	16	Q20
Yealmpton *Devon*	3	X16
Yelverton *Devon*	3	X15
Yeovil *Som'set*	4	W18
Yetminster *Dorset*	4	W18
York *C/York*	16	Q21
Youghal *Cork*	39	U8
Youlgreave *Derby*	11	R20
Yoxall *Staffs*	11	S20
Yoxford *Suffolk*	13	T27
Ysbyty Ifan *Conwy*	8	R16
Ysbyty Ystwyth *Ceredig'n*	9	T16
Ystalyfera *Neath P Talb*	9	U16
Ystradgynlais *Powys*	9	U16

Z

Zennor *Cornw'l*	2	X12